A GIRL'S GUIDE TO
JOINING THE RESISTANCE

A GIRL'S GUIDE TO
JOINING THE RESISTANCE

○ ○ ○ ○ ○ ○ ○ ○ ○ ○ ○ ○ ○

A Feminist Handbook on Fighting for Good

EMMA GRAY

ILLUSTRATED BY EVA HILL

WILLIAM MORROW

An Imprint of HarperCollins*Publishers*

HarperCollins books may be purchased for educational, business, or sales promotional use. For information, please email the Special Markets Department at SPsales@harpercollins.com.

FIRST EDITION

DESIGNED BY LEAH CARLSON-STANISIC

Library of Congress Cataloging-in-Publication Data has been applied for.

ISBN 978-0-06-274808-9

18 19 20 21 22   LSC   10 9 8 7 6 5 4 3 2 1

TO ALL THE GIRLS WHO HAVE BEEN,
ARE, AND WILL BE BRAVE ENOUGH TO
FIGHT FOR OTHER GIRLS

CONTENTS

CONTENTS

INTRODUCTION

On the evening of November 22, 1909, several thousand garment workers squeezed into Cooper Union's Great Hall in New York City. The crowd was almost all women, many still in their teens.

They were there to discuss the poor working conditions that plagued their industry—low wages, inhumane hours, abusive and unsafe environments—and whether they should call for a general strike among shirtwaist makers. This meeting was the culmination of a series of smaller strikes organized by female labor activists, several of which had led to arrests and violence against the picketing workers. The speakers slated for that evening included labor leaders such as the American Federation of Labor's Samuel Gompers, the Women's Trade Union League's Leonora O'Reilly, and B. Feigenbaum of the *Jewish Daily Forward*.[1] One after another, they expressed solidarity with the shirtwaist makers, talking at length about the terrible conditions the workers experienced, while failing to offer concrete actions.

Eventually, a slight twenty-three-year-old Ukrainian Jewish woman named Clara Lemlich—erroneously described by reporters as a teenager, despite already being an experienced organizer—could stand it no longer.

"I want to say a few words," she yelled out, before delivering a short, powerful speech in Yiddish.

"I have listened to all the speakers. I would not have further patience for talk, as I am one of those who feels and suffers from the things pictured. I move that we go on a general strike."

And they did.

The next morning 15,000 shirtwaist makers went on strike.[2] By night, that number had grown to 20,000. Some estimate that as many as 40,000 shirtwaist makers eventually joined the movement.

This strike, known alternately as the Uprising of the 20,000 and (my personal favorite) the Revolt of the Girls,[3] gave energy to the organizing efforts of women garment workers across the country. Within the year, thousands of women workers had gone on strike, from Philadelphia to Chicago. The eleven-week-long Uprising of the 20,000 didn't get the strikers all of their demands, but it did result in concrete progress: 339 waist and dress manufacturers signed contracts granting shorter workweeks, paid holidays, wage negotiations, and a promise not to discriminate against unionized workers.[4]

In 1954,[5] Lemlich, who remained an activist throughout her life, gave an interview about her early days as a labor organizer. "What did I know about trade unionism?" she said. "Audacity—that was all I had—audacity!"

The 2016 presidential election felt, in some ways, like a referendum on the value of women (and people of color and immigrants and refugees and Muslims . . . the list goes on), one that we had lost. On the evening of

November 9, I walked in a daze under the gray, drizzly haze that seemed to permeate New York City to meet three friends, all women who shared my single-minded desire to sit in a cozy, dark corner and plot the resistance—or at the very least feel a modicum of usefulness.

En route to the meet-up, I passed Cooper Union, which stands just around the corner from my office—the site of Clara Lemlich's speech, the place where she had refused to be silent and allow inaction 107 years before.

In the months following the presidential election, I found myself thinking a lot about women like Clara—women who had the audacity to speak out and organize for change before it was possible to rally the masses with a viral hashtag or even cast a vote at the ballot box.

American history is filled with women who slowly but surely transformed the country. But since men's stories are the ones that tend to dominate our history books, we hear less about the contributions of these extraordinary women.

Women such as civil rights leader Diane Nash, who cofounded the Student Nonviolent Coordinating Committee (SNCC) and was instrumental in organizing sit-ins and Freedom Rides to protest segregation in the South.

Or Sarah and Angelina Grimké, white Quaker sisters and abolitionists, who were the first women to testify on the issue of black American rights before a state legislature.[6] They spent much of their lives speaking publicly against slavery, even debating men—something that was nearly unheard of at the time.

Or Sylvia Rivera,[7] who at the age of seventeen was one of the drag queens who fought back against police when they came to raid the Stonewall Inn, helping start the seminal 1969 Stonewall riots. According to the *New York Times*, as the riot began, Sylvia yelled: "I'm not missing a minute of this—it's the revolution!"

Or human rights and antiracism activist and author Grace Lee Boggs, the daughter of Chinese immigrants, who grew up to adopt the teachings of Dr. Martin Luther King Jr. and hosted Malcolm X at her Detroit home.

As OG feminist icon Gloria Steinem once said: "Power can be taken, but not given. The process of the taking is empowerment in itself."[8] Each one of these trailblazing women took power where none was bestowed.

Today women are getting to watch that "process of the taking" play out right in front of their eyes. Necessitated by a political moment that is distinctly hostile to women's rights, women are leading the resistance—from the courts to the streets to Hollywood to the halls of Congress.

Senators such as Kamala Harris, Elizabeth Warren, and Kirsten Gillibrand are persisting like the "nasty women" they are. Alicia Garza, Opal Tometi, and Patrisse Cullors—the women behind Black Lives Matter—are channeling their movement's energy into combating an administration's open disdain for black and brown lives.[9] Women's March national cochairs Tamika Mallory, Linda Sarsour, Bob Bland, and Carmen Perez are turning the massive energy the world witnessed on January 21, 2017, into a movement with true staying power.

And it's not just the most visible leaders of this resistance that matter. Not only has progressive activism surged overall since November 2016, but women are more likely than their male counterparts to write and call Congress, march and protest, and express an intention to get more involved in

the coming years.[10] American women of all ages are showing up and doing the work and giving a fuck.

This book is for the women and girls who give *all* the fucks, because there have always been women and girls who did—women and girls who showed up to fight for their own inalienable rights and the rights of others. This book is for every woman who has chosen to give a fuck despite the odds being stacked against her.

I learned so much from listening to the women I spoke to while writing this book. I hope these pages can serve as a beginner's guide to getting involved—or at least a crash refresher course. (Writing it certainly was for me.) You'll learn steps you can take to start making a tangible difference and how to stay (at least relatively) sane while doing it. And you'll get all this advice from women who live and breathe what they are talking about every damn day, women who have the audacity today that Clara Lemlich had in 1909.

In April 1912, Clara Lemlich argued passionately for working women's right to vote. "We are here, and we are here to stay," she said.

Today, *we* are here. And *we* are here to stay.

So, dear reader, go forth and change the world. There's an army of women who came before you, and they all have your back.

Part One

WELCOME TO THE
RESISTANCE

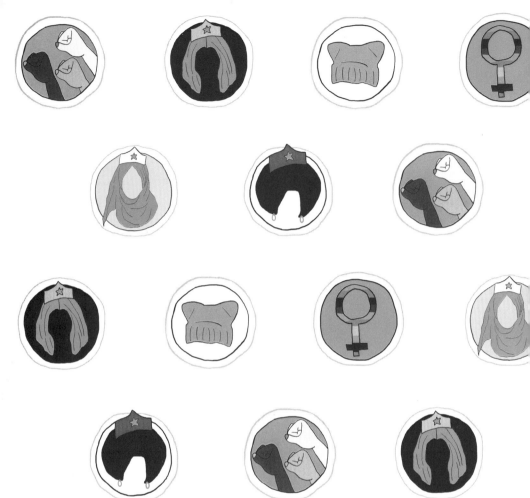

CHAPTER 1

○ ○ ○ ○ ○ ○ ○

THERE'S NO TIME LIKE THE PRESENT TO
GIVE ALL THE F**KS

"If not now, when?"

—HILLEL THE ELDER

When I asked Black Lives Matter cofounder Alicia Garza what would happen if Americans didn't wake up and get active, she didn't mince words.

"If we don't collectively get active in defense of safety and justice for all of us, a lot of us will reap the consequences—including death," she said. "No one is coming to save us except for us, so we might as well get to work."

That's a sentiment I heard echoed by many of the activists I spoke to for this book. The time for action is now—yesterday, really—and if you are a person who cares about your own future, the future of the people around you, and the future of your nation, it's your responsibility to roll up your metaphorical sleeves and jump into the fray.

Of course, this can be easier said than done. It's scary and overwhelming to think about how much is at stake: access to health care, abortion rights, voting rights, the physical safety of trans people when they walk down the street, the physical safety of black Americans when they interact with police, and, ya know, the survival of the entire freaking earth.

The first months of Donald Trump's presidency provided a litany of examples of what can happen when a white supremacist agenda makes its way into the White House. The following are just a handful:

- Travel bans targeting Muslim-majority countries were issued.

- The GOP attempted to do some combination of repealing and replacing the Affordable Care Act, which left up to 32 million people vulnerable to losing health insurance[1] over less than ten years.[2]
- The president pulled back protections for women workers.[2]
- The president touted what he labeled[3] a "military operation" to identify, arrest, and deport undocumented immigrants.
- A guidance protecting transgender students in public schools was rescinded.
- A budget was proposed that cut funding for PBS, the National Endowment for the Arts, and Meals on Wheels.
- The president pulled the United States out of the Paris climate agreement.
- The global gag rule[4] was drastically expanded, prohibiting any global health funding for organizations that provide or even mention abortion as an option to women.

- An Obama-era rule[5] that prohibited mentally ill individuals from purchasing guns was rolled back.
- The president signed a measure that allows states to withhold Title X funding for family planning from clinics that provide abortions.
- The president issued a memo directing the Pentagon to ban transgender people from openly serving in the U.S. military.

Let's play a ~~fun~~ terrifying game and try to name a few of the groups that stood to be impacted by those decisions: trans kids, undocumented immigrants, documented immigrants, Muslim Americans, public school students, children who watch *Sesame Street*, poor senior citizens, artists, women who need birth control, women who need maternity care, anyone who needs health care at some point in their lives and can't afford to pay thousands of dollars every time they access it, all Americans who would prefer the United States protect its national security interests, people who are looking to spend some quality time on planet Earth. That covers a hell of a lot of people.

"This is a time to define the values our country stands for, and to fight for those values," Tina Tchen, former chief of staff to First Lady Michelle Obama and executive director of the Obama White House Council on Women and Girls, told me, "like caring for those in need, expanding social justice for all, and protecting our planet for future generations. The beauty of our democratic system is that these choices are in the hands of the people, citizens who can make their voices, and their votes, heard."

And during those first months of Trump's presidency, we witnessed what a difference it makes when people are paying attention and taking a stand. The Women's March(es) across the country became the largest single-day demonstration in U.S. history.[6] People showed up en masse to protest at airports within hours of Trump's initial sweeping travel ban. Citizens came to town halls and flooded their elected officials' offices with calls, creating political roadblocks for a GOP-controlled Congress that wanted to swiftly repeal and replace the Affordable Care Act. Thousands of women expressed interest in running for office.[7]

Collective action makes a difference—we've seen it happen.

When you are a member of a group whose basic rights and safety are generally protected, it can be easy to ignore that the rights and safety of your fellow citizens *are not*. This cushion of security can make it seem to some of us like politics is something that can be separated from ourselves and our lives.

For some Americans, the election was a clarifying moment. For some, specifically middle- and upper-class progressive white people, a long-treasured vision of this country as unified and fundamentally open-minded was dashed.

It's not that our nation actually transformed overnight, though in some circles it certainly felt like it had. It's more that the fury and resentment and tribalism that had long existed within communities that felt ignored and threatened—helped along by healthy doses of xenophobia, Islamophobia, racism, and sexism—had come bubbling up to the surface and into our country's voting booths. It's far harder to ignore all the underlying inequalities that make up American society when a walking, talking, pussy-grabbing orange caricature of incompetent toxic masculinity is its face.

"I think a lot of silver spoons were pulled out of mouths, and now people are understanding that they can't take their happiness or their health care or the political process for granted," organizer and writer Raquel Willis told me.

Of course, those silver spoons were only in the mouths of people born white and straight and cisgender and financially secure—people like me.

"The truth is that there were always people fighting," Raquel continued. "Thinking about the most marginalized—people of color, black folks, poor folks, disabled folks, trans folks, queer folks, and women. We've been fighting. It's only now that I think people are starting to understand that [the reason] we haven't been more successful is because we weren't invested in the liberation of those other marginalized folks as much as we should have been."

Guilty as charged. I certainly have had moments where I preferred to dissociate a little bit, to push aside the knowledge that people are hurting every day in this country, because it feels hard and confusing and scary to really sit with that understanding. Maybe you've also had those moments . . . or days . . . or weeks . . . or years.

Set whatever you haven't done in the past aside, and get looking toward the future. Remember that guilt is a useless emotion—one that often sinks us deeper into a hole of inaction rather than pulling us out of it and lighting a fire under our asses. Deciding that you are powerless is also useless. The important thing is that you're ready to show up now.

Maybe that future includes raising money for organizations that you believe in. Maybe it includes going door to door campaigning for someone you believe will do good if elected to office. Maybe it means making sure you're informed about local elections, and that you become a more active participant in democracy. Maybe it includes showing up to protests in solidarity with communities you're not currently connected to. Maybe it includes pushing your local school district to broaden its sex education. Maybe it includes putting pressure on the education secretary to keep and enforce protections for victims of college sexual assault. Maybe it includes setting five minutes aside each day to call your congressperson. Maybe it includes running for office yourself.

"When people sit on the sidelines in our democracy and let others set the terms of political debates, then they surrender the policy decisions to the biggest corporations and billionaires who can hire armies of lawyers and lobbyists," said Senator Elizabeth Warren when I asked her why acting now is so important. "In that case, our country will keep working better and better for a smaller and smaller number of people. It's up to us to make sure that doesn't happen."

That "us" is you, dear reader. No matter who you are, there's not a moment to waste. Use your time, brilliance, money—and fire tweets—for good.

CHAPTER 2

○ ○ ○ ○ ○ ○ ○

HEY GIRL(S) HEY:
WHY YOUNG WOMEN'S VOICES ARE SO DAMN
ESSENTIAL

Being a woman means growing up in a world that tells you to be quiet in a million small ways every day.

The messages are subtle, of course, but omnipresent. Don't be too big. Don't be too small. Don't be too young. Don't be too old. Don't try too hard. Don't be too loud. Don't take up too much space. Be successful but not threatening. Be beautiful but naturally so. Buy all the things that corporations tell you will help you conform to these impossible standards, but don't make it obvious that you needed any products to achieve "perfection." And while you're spinning out trying to be the thing that you think you must be to be worthwhile, the men around you are free to learn, to speak, to explore, to lead.

It's easy to say that we should all just say "screw that" and take up space anyway. And... we should! But the reality is that it's way easier said than done.

TO BE
WORTHWHILE

Motivation and engagement take work. They take constant reaffirmation and reminding of why these fights are so damn important. When my own faith is failing me or weakening, I turn to the greatest teachers I know: other women.

I asked the women I spoke to for this book why we need young women's voices in this fight. Every answer was beautiful, and I want them all printed on motivational posters to hang on my wall (maybe an Etsy store is in my future?). But instead of doing that, I decided to put them all in one place for you, dear reader.

CARMEN PEREZ, Women's March National Cochair

"Women are the ones who are the driving forces in many of the issues that we care about. Women are at the forefront. They've always been at the forefront. It's important for us to nurture young people because young people have always led movements. When we look at SNCC [the Student Nonviolent Coordinating Committee], when we look at the Chicano movement or the American Indian movement, it was young people. And so the way in which I see change is by cultivating the leadership of youth, and specifically young women, so that they can be the agents [of change] in their own families and in their own communities. I see myself in a lot of the young girls that I work with, but the difference between them and myself is that I was given an opportunity and they weren't. So that's what I really try to do: give young women opportunities to have access to leadership development or civic engagement or political engagement."

MARLO THOMAS, Award-Winning Actress, Author, and Activist

"It is up to [young women] now to carry the fight forward, as these issues will define their lives and their children's lives. Today's young women are the ones whose reproductive rights are most dangerously under siege. They are the ones carrying student debt into a workforce that still doesn't pay them fairly in many states. And God knows, they and all young people are the ones who will be most imperiled by whatever environmental damage the planet will suffer in the next half century. But in spite of all these challenges, I feel optimistic—because as someone who participates as much as I can in social media, I am continually inspired by the intelligence and relentlessness of today's young women warriors. They are keeping us all on the leading edge of modern feminism, and I am learning from them every day."

LUCY McBATH, Mother of the Movement, Spokesperson for Moms Demand Action for Gun Sense in America, and Faith Outreach Leader for Everytown for Gun Safety

"The young women of today are the mothers of tomorrow. It's about preserving your own futures. It's about protecting your families. Young women are going to be mothers. They're going to be community leaders, and they're going to be active in their churches and community organizations. I tell young people all the time that I'm fifty-seven but I'm out there fighting for you. We need you to fight for you."

PAT SCHROEDER, Former Congresswoman

"If you're going to make democracy work, you've got to work at democracy and social justice. In 2020, women in this country will have had the vote for one hundred years. Equal pay, the obsession with trying to control women's reproductive rights—things like that should be over with. We should have moved on, and women should be in positions of leadership, and yet in 2017 you just see the Senate deciding there would be thirteen people negotiating the [GOP

Senate] health care bill, and they couldn't bother to put a woman senator in there. You're just seeing that every single day. We certainly have the education, we have the ability. It's never too late for equal rights."

AMANDA GORMAN, Activist and Youth Poet Laureate of the United States

"Young female and femme voices are so vital because they add more to the narrative that is often left untold, and just sociologically speaking, we also see that people who identify as women have a good capacity for collaboration, for empathy, for reaching across the aisles. And while I'll always be afraid of people using those stereotypes as a way to limit women, I think the strength of identifying as a woman, whether you're cisgender or trans, it gives you this interesting perspective into not only patriarchy in the United States but also other systems of oppression. One woman can tap into that as a united force, [and] we see an earthquake that rocks the world."

SARAH McBRIDE, National Press Secretary for the Human Rights Campaign and LGBTQ Activist

"I can't underscore enough the importance of young voices in these conversations. Young voices are going to be the voices that inherit this environment, and are learning in our schools, and are gonna be entering the job force. So they have a real stake in the policy discussions that we're having. But beyond that, they're so necessary because they're incredibly effective voices for the types of progressive change we need. When they speak on political issues, they are speaking from a place of history. Young people will be the ones who write the history books of tomorrow. And elected officials, business leaders, and the everyday public—they know that."

JACKIE CRUZ, Actress and Activist

"All young people need to engage right now in social justice issues. They're our future—particularly women. We need to learn from a young age the importance of civil engagement, standing up for our rights, and having our voices heard. It starts as young as [immigration rights activist] Sophie Cruz. I mean, she's six years old."

GABRIELLE GORMAN, Filmmaker and YoungArts Winner

"I always like to refer back to this pep talk that I saw. [The woman giving the talk] is talking about the danger of the single story that's only heard from a particular perspective, a particular group of people. That's why female voices are so important—and to have a diverse range of female voices, people from different sexualities, people from different communities and cultures. I think it's important to recognize that intersectionality."

ELIZABETH WARREN, United States Senator

"If not you, then who? If not now, then when? We need more women to speak up and make their voices heard. We need you in this fight."

AI-JEN POO, Director of the National Domestic Workers Alliance and Codirector of Caring Across Generations

"Women are often talked about as a special interest group, but we are more than half of all college graduates, more than half the electorate. We are doing 70 percent of the caregiving work, and we are more than 70 percent of all consumers, so our experiences and our perspectives are more defining of the whole than ever. So our perspectives need to be at the table to design solutions that actually work. Because if you're not looking at the world through the eyes of women, you're not seeing the whole picture."

SHANNON WATTS, Founder of Moms Demand Action for Gun Sense in America

"Women are the secret sauce. Women are what make organizing go. Incorporating women's ability to be compassionate and passionate and multitask is key to winning and organizing. If you look at the front line of activism for so long—child labor laws, drunk driving, the right to vote—there are so many different areas that you can demonstrate where women have been leading the charge."

WENDY DAVIS, Former State Senator and Founder of Deeds Not Words

"We need more women, period [in the fight for social justice], but I think we have the greatest potential lift in getting the voices of young women to be part of the conversation simply by virtue of the percentage of the population that young women occupy. By the year 2020, millennials as a whole, women and men, are going to be 40 percent of the eligible voters in this country. If we were able to really turn on the power that young women and young men possess, we would change the dynamic completely of what the conversation is in political contests and in policy making."

JANAYE INGRAM, National Organizer and Head of Logistics for Women's March

"Movements have always been led by young people. I think that there is a certain impatience that comes with being young. We are the microwave generation, where everything happens in an instant. You can talk to someone halfway across the world in a click of a button. You can get your food in five minutes, and it's completely cooked. Everything just happens so fast. Because of that, I think that that impatience has also bled into our understanding of social injustice. We want to see change, and we are going to fight to make that happen. Young people, we can go out, and we can stand in the streets all night, like they did in Ferguson [following the shooting of Michael Brown by white police officer Darren Wilson]. We can stay out all night and do that, days upon days upon days on end. The elders, their responsibility is to guide us, and to engage us, and to tell us how we can better strategize, what lessons they learned."

DEJA FOXX, High School Student and Reproductive Justice Advocate

"I would encourage other young women to speak their truth and share their experiences, [because] their stories are agents of change. Young people, women, LGBTQ folks, and people of color must be at the forefront of our movements. The future leaders are those who come from diverse backgrounds, and it is time that we take that role up and defy the systematic forces that for so long have held us back. We are the future!"

BOB BLAND, Women's March National Cochair

"You know the phrase 'The future is female'? It's not just a phrase; it's not just a tag line to sell shirts. It is really the truth. And the reason why it's so important to have women and girls centered in leadership in all these conversations is, first of all, because it's the one thing we haven't tried. You know, patriarchy had a good run. We've been doing this for what, a few millennia? And what have we gotten from that? We've gotten war, we've gotten competition, we've gotten capitalism brought to its most sociopathic and extreme. Women have not had the chance to take the lead. And that is why we must now. I remember when Dr. Bernice King was speaking to all of our [Women's March] organizers in December [2016]. She quoted her mother, Coretta Scott King, and she said, 'First of all, women, if the soul of the nation is to be saved, I think you must become its soul.' Women must give birth to whatever the new generation of this country and this society is to become, because we are the connector of everything. Every single person on this earth has something in common with each other. It's that every single person came out of a woman. There are so many things that divide us, but that is an undeniable fact. And it's powerful that we are tasked with bringing life into this world."

ALICIA GARZA, Cofounder of Black Lives Matter Network and Special Projects Director at the National Domestic Workers Alliance

"Young women's voices are needed in the fight for social justice because there's so much happening in the world right now that directly impacts women and girls. I look at the photos coming out of the White House these days with a zillion white men sitting around a table making decisions about women's bodies, our health, and our lives, and it is completely infuriating. There are hardly any women at the table, if any at all. And then if we were to look at the racial and ethnic compositions of those rooms where decisions are being made, they are pale and male. Young women deserve to make decisions that are best for us, and there's no better time than now to get involved. Otherwise, the health care we need to have safe and healthy families, the communities we desire where children could grow up to become adults and be free of violence, will never materialize."

SARAH SOPHIE FLICKER, National Organizer for Women's March, **Creative Director and Performer**

"Young people just get it. I definitely feel like the smartest thing I do for my activism is hang out with people younger than I am and really allow them to lead. I really enjoy their voices, and I feel like I learn new things all the time. That's just the obvious, inevitable way that progress happens. If you look at people who are real leaders, like Gloria Steinem, for example, she really knows how to listen. She really values all the younger people coming up. She does not try to tell them what's what."

TINA TCHEN, Former Chief of Staff to First Lady Michelle Obama and **Executive Director of the Obama White House Council on Women and Girls**

"Young women are living lives of inclusion and are fighting for a future with social justice and equal opportunity for all. They are working on creative and innovative solutions. They are resilient and they are powerful. They understand the complexity of opportunity and access, and what it means to have limits on that just because of identity. Most of all, it is their future that is at stake right now and the voices of young women are critical to shaping that future."

ASHLEY JUDD, Actor, Author, and Activist

"Young people offer fresh thinking, stamina, and a necessary rowdiness. They also have a grasp of existing and emerging technologies and how they continue to revolutionize our world, and they will use them for social movements in ways that those of us who are older can't begin to envision but will eventually embrace. What's blatantly obvious is that we currently have the largest youth cohort the planet has ever known. It is a young person's world. With Hillary [Clinton] recently running for president of the United States and being so eminently qualified, there are fortunately now generations of young women and girls who don't know that was novel, relative to our nation's long history of the white man's stranglehold on power and politics."

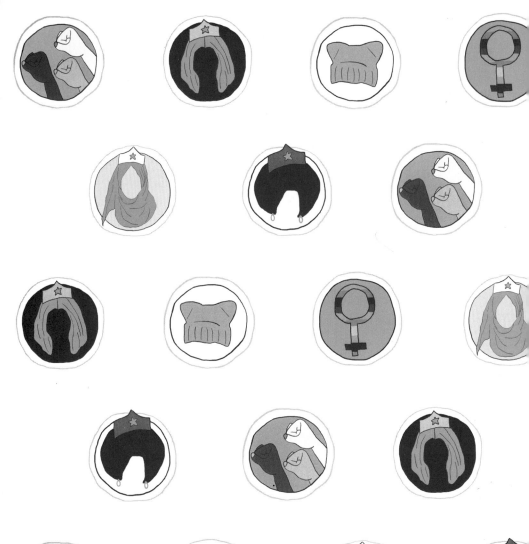

CHAPTER 3

∘ ∘ ∘ ∘ ∘ ∘ ∘

ON GETTING ANGRY:
THE POWER OF PROTEST

On March 25, 1993, Congresswoman Pat Schroeder stood on a podium in front of hundreds of thousands of LGBTQ people and their allies in Washington, DC. This crowd was gathered with a list of clear demands, among them, government action on the AIDS crisis, a lift of the ban on gay people serving in the military, and legislation to protect LGBTQ families.

"Remember as we stand in this great capital of this wonderful nation, when we say the pledge of allegiance, we say 'with liberty and justice for all,'" Schroeder declared. "Well, what part of 'all' don't people understand? We mean *all*."

The *New York Times* described the tone of this march—the March on Washington for Lesbian, Gay, and Bi Equal Rights and Liberation—as "one of pride, of feeling part of a larger gay community and not being afraid to march down the street to proclaim it," and commented that "many marchers were accompanied by small children and parents."[1] I was one of those children.

I'm not sure if this was the first protest or march I ever attended, but it's certainly the first one I can remember. I was five years old, and from where I was sitting—in my younger brother's stroller, being pushed by a rotating cast of my mother, my father, and my grandma—it looked joyful, a crowded downtown DC filled with colorful people and rainbow flags and shirtless women wearing stickers to cover their nipples. (I remember being particularly curious about that.) In the one photo I have from that day,[2] I'm holding a rainbow flag in my hand, peeking out from underneath a painfully nineties neon-blue hat. My grandmother is wearing a PFLAG sash, and a smiling woman with a cropped haircut in the background is holding up a sign that reads, simply, LESBIAN RIGHTS.

It's unclear how much I actually understood about what was going on that day, but something about the magic of being in a crowd unified by common purpose and love and anger made it into my subconscious. I've been to many protests and marches since that one, first as a participant and later as a journalist. And each time I remember again the magic of that collective energy I witnessed at age five. I marched in protest of the Iraq War and in support of Planned Parenthood. I got to interview children and parents who attended Occupy Wall Street's family sleepover in 2012[3]— "I think it's good for kids to participate in democracy," mother of two Megan Davidson told me at the time. "This is what democracy looks like." I got to document New York City's first marches in solidarity with Black Lives Matter. And on January 21, 2017, I was back in Washington, DC, witnessing history—or, rather, *her*story—at the Women's March.[4]

Along with my coworkers Alanna, Catherine, and Damon, I spent the day weaving through the crowds, speaking to women, men, and children about why they were out there—on that day, in that place, together. Every person who took the time to talk to us had a moving

reason, but one eighty-three-year-old woman, who had shown up with her cane and her three girlfriends clad in custom pink NASTY (OLD) WOMAN sweatshirts, made a lasting impression.

Susan had been in the protest game for decades. She had shown up for her black brothers and sisters in the 1960s, at the height of the civil rights movement. "I marched from Selma to Montgomery," she told me, "and I truly believe in the energy and the spirit of mass protest."

☆　　☆　　☆

That date of that march, March 7, 1965, came to be known as "Bloody Sunday,"[5] for the brutal and televised police violence used against protesters on the Edmund Pettus Bridge in Selma, Alabama.

The Student Nonviolent Coordinating Committee (SNCC) had been working to register black voters around Selma for months and facing great resistance from the state government and law enforcement. In February of 1965 a police officer shot twenty-six-year-old activist Jimmie Lee Jackson as he rushed over to help his mother during a peaceful civil rights demonstration. About a week later, on February 26, Jackson died. In response, the march from Selma to Montgomery (the capital of Alabama) was planned.[6]

Many are familiar with the key male players of that march and the marches that followed: Dr. Martin Luther King Jr., of course; now-congressman John Lewis, James Bevel, Hosea Williams. But women activists were also a key driving force: Diane Nash, Amelia Boynton Robinson, Annie Lee Cooper, Viola Liuzzo, and more.

For Diane Nash, who was twenty-six when Bloody Sunday took place, the impetus behind the march from Selma to Montgomery came earlier than 1965. Around the fiftieth anniversary of Bloody Sunday, she remembered the 1963 Ku Klux Klan bombing of a Baptist church in Alabama, which resulted in the deaths of four young black girls.

"The day the girls were murdered in the bombing at the Sixteenth Street Baptist Church in Birmingham, [then-husband James Bevel] and I wrote the initial plan for what became the Selma Right to Vote movement," she told a local ABC news station[7] in March 2015.

For several years she and James tried to convince Dr. King to join them in Alabama. Eventually they succeeded.

On that fateful Sunday, some six hundred demonstrators marched through downtown Selma to the Edmund Pettus Bridge, named for a Confederate general. Halfway across, they saw a human wall of state troopers on the other side, as white locals looked on.

The *New York Times* described what happened next:[8]

The scene in Selma resembled that in a police state. Heavily armed men attacked the marchers. [. . .] Tear gas was used. [. . .] Witnesses "said they saw possemen using whips on the fleeing Negroes as they recrossed the bridge." If this is described as law enforcement, it is mis-named. It is nothing more nor less than race-conscious officialdom run amuck. It disgraces not only the state of Alabama but every citizen of the country in which it can happen.

The video footage of this brutal altercation—and the peaceful response of the protesters who were being attacked—was broadcast across the nation, leading to more marches, more violence, and widespread outcry.

Eventually, the protests succeeded and the Voting Rights Act, which prohibits racial discrimination in voting and removed barriers to registration such as poll taxes and literacy tests, was signed into law by President Lyndon Johnson on August 6, 1965 (sadly in 2013 essential parts of the VRA were gutted by the Supreme Court).

While Diane is widely recognized as a leader in the civil rights movement, and was immortalized in the Ava Duvernay–helmed film *Selma*, she has always been careful to point out that the fight for civil rights depended on a movement rather than an individual.

"It took many thousands of people to make the changes that we've made," she said in 2015. "People whose names we'll never know. They'll never get credit for the sacrifices they've made, but I remember them."

☆ ☆ ☆

Public acts of resistance are effective because they can more easily be amplified by passersby and the media. One person on a street corner can go unnoticed—or at least be tuned out. But get fifty or five hundred or five thousand or fifty thousand people together, all unified around one issue, and they become a hell of a lot harder to ignore.

Today's resistance is fueled by collective action—on social media, at town halls, in the streets. Collective, or at the very least coordinated, actions tend to receive media coverage, and media coverage makes it easier to hold elected officials' feet to the fire. Momentum begets momentum.

But when you don't have fifty thousand (or even five hundred) people in one place, deploying your voice wisely can suffice. In an era dominated by 24/7 TV and web news coverage, as well as social media, getting your voice heard is far easier. (Any girl with a Twitter or Instagram account understands that.)

Look no further than Deja Foxx. Just days before her seventeenth birthday, the Tuscon, Arizona, teen showed up at Republican senator Jeff Flake's April 2017 town hall with a question: "Why would you deny me the American dream if Planned Parenthood is helping me reach it?"

Less than a week prior, Senator Flake had voted to allow states to block Title X family-planning funding for health care providers that also perform abortions—such as Planned Parenthood. (The Hyde Amendment already prevents federal Medicaid coverage for abortion services unless a woman's life is in danger, or in cases of rape and incest.) Foxx, along with many other Arizonans, showed up to speak to Flake when he returned to his home state.

"I just want to state some facts," she told the senator. "I'm a young woman; you're a middle-aged man. I'm a person of color, and you're white. I come from a background of poverty, and I didn't always have parents to guide me through life; you come from privilege. I'm wondering, as a Planned Parenthood patient and someone who relies on Title X, who you are clearly not, why is it your right to take away my right to choose Planned Parenthood?"[9]

Her questions were met with huge cheers and applause from the other constituents gathered. Mere hours later, the video footage of her exchange with Senator Flake went viral, because, quite simply, Deja is a total badass. Her questions were pointed, personal, and effective—and Senator Flake responded with meaningless platitudes.

When I spoke to Deja, the week after her exchange with the senator, she told me that she's always had the spirit of activism in her life but that she had really begun getting involved in more formal organizing when she joined the fight for comprehensive sex ed in her Arizona school district. And which organization provided mentorship and leadership trainings for her and her peers? Planned Parenthood.

For Deja, the fight for sex education and birth control access felt personal.

"That fight was especially personal for me because, without parents, I relied on my school to provide me with factual, medically accurate, and updated information to help me make educated decisions about my future," she said. "It became even more personal as I watched my peers grow as leaders in the process, and I felt a real sense of pride in having taken part in empowering them. That sense of pride and goal of empowerment is what encourages me to continue fighting."

The fight against injustice will always be long and often discouraging. The only way to persist is to choose a cause you feel that your life—and the lives of others—depends on, one you can speak to from (for lack of a better, less cheesy phrase) the heart. There's a reason that thousands of people showed up to town halls across the country to express their displeasure with the GOP health care plan(s) and to demand that their elected officials not try to take away health care from poor and middle-class people. Those stories created change.

"Small acts of resistance when done by many people are the seeds of solidarity," Deja told me. "Standing united and experiencing compassion when faced with the struggles and stories of others is what makes us stronger in the face of divisive political force."

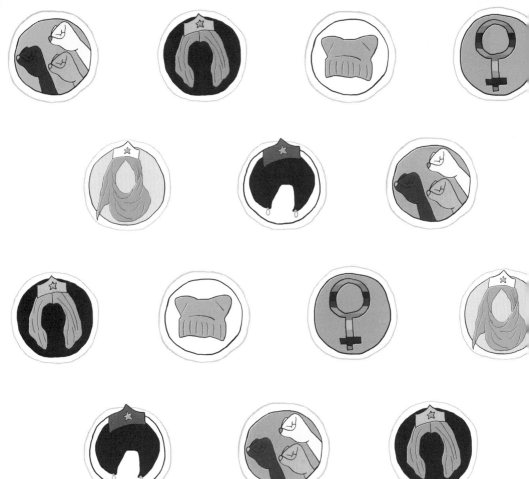

CHAPTER 4

○ ○ ○ ○ ○ ○ ○

DEAR WHITE LADIES:
A NOTE ON INTERSECTIONALITY

"My feminism will be intersectional or it will be bullshit."

—FLAVIA DZODAN, TIGER BEATDOWN

The first time I heard the term *intersectionality*, I was in college. Surprise, surprise, the lady who ended up writing about women's issues professionally spent four years discussing the merits of Judith Butler and bell hooks. Shocking, right? But I know that I felt relieved to finally have a word to describe a concept that felt totally integral to everything I was learning (and living).

At its core, intersectionality is simple, almost obvious: groups of people are not monolithic—our identities overlap and compound in myriad ways. Therefore, when you talk about "women" or "the LGBTQ community," you are talking about groups of people who share some common experiences but whose lives vary in many other ways. The key is that these differences impact the way that individuals experience the world and therefore the way they experience whatever particular oppression an activist or organizer is trying to combat. If you are blind to—or willfully ignore—these differences, it becomes impossible to create lasting and meaningful solutions; if a solution addresses only a *part* of the problem, it's not actually a solution at all—it's a Band-Aid, reserved for only a few.

LGBTQIA

As gun-safety activist Lucy McBath put it, "You cannot focus on one issue without the intersectionality of all of the issues. It's like you have a wheel and every issue is a spoke that ties into that wheel. Until we're able to eradicate or work on all of these kinds of issues, we'll never solve one issue. Because they're all intricately connected."

You might be thinking, "Well . . . duh." And you'd be right! But putting intersectionality into practice is when things get tough. There's not a social movement in history that hasn't had issues with actually advocating for the entirety of the group it purports to be fighting for. Look no further than the suffragettes, many of whom chose to prioritize middle-class white women's rights at the expense of women of color.[1]

This problematic idea of educated middle-class white women as a universal stand-in for "women" continues to be an issue today. But today we are, at the very least, better equipped to confront it.

In my experience, most young women already understand these concepts—or latch onto them quickly once introduced to them. They understand intersectionality and white feminism, which is more than I can say for my own teenage self. Young women today *know* that feminism without intersectionality is no feminism at all.

☆　☆　☆

Intersectionality theory was first named by law professor Kimberlé Crenshaw in the 1980s to address a specific issue: the compounding and overlapping discrimination that women of color face in the workforce, and the failure of anti-discrimination laws—which looked at race and gender discrimination as completely separate entities rather than overlapping and compounding—to address that reality.[2]

In the more general sense, intersectionality is a lens and analytical tool through which to view the world holistically. It points to the varying and complex ways that different facets of our identities intersect, informing the oppression that we experience. A black woman is not going to experience sexism in the exact same way as a white woman. A butch, queer, Latina woman is not going to experience homophobia the same way a bisexual, femme, Asian woman does. And all of the corresponding isms and phobias ultimately serve the same common purpose: to keep most of us divided and down in order to lift up a vaunted few (a.k.a., able-bodied, affluent, straight, cisgender white men). And it's historically been a reluctance—primarily by affluent, straight, cisgender white women—to acknowledge these differences and intersections that has created the erasure of many women in feminist spaces.

This is a reality that self-described "proud, unapologetic, queer, black, transgender woman from Augusta, Georgia" Raquel Willis spoke about at the Women's March, nodding to the iconic "Ain't I a Woman" speech women's rights and antislavery activist Sojourner Truth gave at the 1851 Women's Convention in Ohio.

"I want to stress the importance of us being intentional about inclusion," Willis said to the thousands gathered in DC. "Black women, women of color, queer women, trans women, disabled women, Muslim women, and so many others are still asking many of y'all, 'Ain't I a woman?' So as we commit to build this movement of resistance and liberation, no one can be an afterthought."

This idea has been key to the broadening of the feminist movement, especially in pushing white feminists to consider the many ways that race and gender interact. Because white feminism (that is, feminism by and for white women only, which doesn't consider the nuanced experiences that women have depending on their varying identities) isn't true feminism.

As Crenshaw put it during a 2014 interview: "Intersectionality draws attention to invisibilities that exist in feminism, in antiracism, in class politics, so . . . it takes a lot of work to consistently challenge ourselves to be attentive to aspects of power that we don't ourselves experience."[3]

The last few years have brought intersectionality solidly out of the academic realm and into the mainstream. Google searches for the term have increased pretty steadily since 2012, shooting up since December 2016, peaking between January 22 and 28, 2017—the week directly following the Women's March.

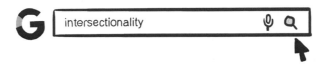

It's no coincidence that Women's March organizers, many of whom are women of color, prioritized intersectionality in the march's platform.[4] The policy platform addressed the gender pay gap, reproductive access, and violence against women, as well as mass incarceration, the Flint water crisis, police brutality, and the rights of LGBTQ people, sex workers, people with disabilities, immigrants, and refugees.

As the authors of the Women's March platform wrote: "Our liberation is bound in each other's."

We cannot fight for women's rights without fighting for racial equality and LGBTQ rights. We cannot battle Islamophobia without battling xenophobia and anti-Semitism and ableism. We rise together or we fall together.

Women of color understand intersectionality because they live and breathe it every day. A lack of intersectionality within social justice movements often means that people of color are ignored, spoken over, and devalued. For those of us who don't experience racial discrimination, being aware of those intersections of identity and experience may take a bit more work. If you're white (and straight and cisgender and able-bodied), you may be able to check out from the struggle sometimes—a privilege that women of color simply don't have. That just means you need to listen, learn, and, as writer Flavia Dzodan stresses, *try*.

Sarah Sophie Flicker, who worked on the Women's March platform, speaks decisively to the particular responsibility that white women have to follow rather than always trying to lead in the fight for social justice. Over coffee, I asked her how women, especially white women, who are just dipping their toes into activism can make sure that intersectionality is an integral part of that activism.

Her advice was pretty simple: listen.

"Linda Sarsour said something that I loved the other day, which is that people who are closest to the problem are often closest to the solution," she told me. "I think a big part of intersectionality and accepting your privilege is just taking a deep breath. Take a beat before you say something. Don't suck the air out of the room. Show up for a community outside your own, but don't try to speak for them. If you have the mic, pass it on if it's someone [else's] story. And that also takes the pressure off of you. You don't need to know everything."

Sarsour's fellow national cochair Bob Bland stressed that as a white woman, planning the Women's March involved a huge amount of learning and listening on her part—particularly about the ugly history of racism within feminist circles.

"I had only heard the term *intersectional* once before," Bland told me. "A lot of the phrases, a lot of the words, a lot of the quotes, a lot of the names—I didn't know any of that before planning the Women's March. And I think it's important for people to know that, not just because it's the truth. But also so that it emboldens women to know that it's okay. You need to start where you are, and if you're committed to intersectionality and if you're committed to justice, then you can learn."

As a white woman, I get an education every day from women of color, and my understanding of how best to practice intersectionality in my daily life—and especially in my work—continues to grow. I asked many of the women I interviewed for this book to tell me what intersectionality meant to them, and how it played out in the work they do. I learned a lot by listening to them—listening is key—and I wanted to share that wisdom with you, dear readers.

Here's what intersectionality means for eighteen active, influential women:

DEJA FOXX, High School Student and Reproductive Justice Advocate

"Intersectionality is really what activism is all about. Our identities and experiences are unique to us, and working to appreciate that in the methods we use to resist oppression makes us more united. To appreciate the intersections of an issue like reproductive justice is to look at the larger machine of oppression and the ways it affects each of us in different ways. But what is most important about this understanding is meeting the experiences of others with compassion."

LUCY McBATH, Mother of the Movement, Spokesperson for Moms Demand Action for Gun Sense in America, and Faith Outreach Leader for Everytown for Gun Safety

"Gun violence prevention is related to systemic racism, poverty, lack of education, mass incarceration, unequal pay for equal work. You cannot work on one issue without it being directly or indirectly related or correlated to any of those issues. When you look at something such as gun violence prevention, you've gotta understand the dynamics of what has helped to create gun violence. Why is there such rampant gun violence, and why is it disproportionately people of color who are affected by gun violence? It's understanding, like I said, poverty, mass incarceration, unlawful police [action]. You cannot focus on one issue without the intersectionality of all of the issues."

JANAYE INGRAM, National Organizer and Head of Logistics for Women's March

"Intersectionality means embracing the cross section of the issues impacting our lives. Whether you're a black woman like me—that's my intersection: I'm black, and I'm a woman—[or] whether you are Latina and a woman who is disabled, the cross section is where your advocacy has to come from. When we go out into the world, when we experience life, we are experiencing these things from the perspective of all of who we are. We don't get to pick and choose,

'Today, I'm going to be black. Today, I'm going to be a woman.' We have to encounter the world from that perspective, and the issues that we're dealing with are because of that cross section, so our advocacy has to be focused and centered in that space. Bringing that to the table also increases the awareness that other people have about those various issues or perspectives.

I have done a lot of work with the disability community. I have been a partner of the disability community in making sure that their voice is heard at the table for the civil rights community. For me, through the process [of planning the Women's March], I had my own discovery of yes, I've been an advocate, yes, I've been an ally, yes, I've been a partner to the disability community, but I still had an opportunity to learn when I was sitting there having these calls with members from the disability community and hearing the various issues. [. . .] The way that we treat the disability community in this country is like lumping together all people of color, just assuming that what one needs, they all need. And that's not the case. [. . .] All of that [is] to say, the intersection of our advocacy is able to inform others and educate others about things that they may not be aware of."

FLAVIA DZODAN, Writer
"[Intersectionality is] a lens through which I look at all political, and social, and cultural issues. I try—I say try, because we all have blind spots, but what I try to do is look at everything from that intersectional lens. To me, it's a tool that you apply trying to understand any given situation. It's an exercise of thinking of the world outside yourself, outside of your own lived reality. I'm specifically thinking here of young white women, because you [don't need] to explain this to young women of color, who have already lived through this. For young white women, it's a matter of thinking outside their own subjectivity."

WINNIE WONG, Founder of People for Bernie
"Intersectionality, to me, on a very practical level means that we are all equal; that there are no walls. We have to move forward and understand that libera-

tion in one person means liberation of all people. When you wake up and when you deal with someone on the street, you cannot think of them as being anyone else other than your neighbor, your brother, or your sister."

AMANDA GORMAN, Activist and Youth Poet Laureate of the United States

"*Intersectionality* is kind of a buzzword, and sometimes if you say a word too much, you forget its meaning. But intersectionality for me, at least in the feminism movement, is a willingness to interrogate [the ways] in which our experiences converge and diverge. And also the commitment to unite for women's rights with that awareness. Young women of today have excavated something that is quite significant and builds upon the work of previous feminists. We're more open to interrogating the intersections of race, gender, class, ability, immigration, et cetera. And that type of critical thinking, which looks at a woman's identity as a mosaic, rather than a one-color painting, I think that is the power behind women and girls of today."

CARMEN PEREZ, Women's March National Cochair

"Intersectionality for me is my own existence as a woman of color. I am intersectional. I grew up in poverty. I also have a family member who's formerly incarcerated, a sister who passed away. As a woman of color, I see my intersectionality being my own existence, being able to navigate in multiple worlds, being able to understand that I'm not monolithic. As women, we're not monolithic. We can care about different things that impact us personally. Having a mother who was from Mexico and a father who was born in the U.S., again, that's being intersectional. It's understanding that we live in multiple worlds."

WENDY DAVIS, Former State Senator and Founder of Deeds Not Words

"Here's how I think about [intersectionality] in terms of gender equality. If you go back to the early 1970s, women were demanding passage of the Equal Rights Amendment, which would have created the backbone against which all of our fights for equality could have been supported. The fact that we weren't able to pass that created a different strategy. It was a strategy that decided we were going to take on issues separately and distinctly, bit by bit, so taking on equality of pay as a distinct issue, access to affordable contraception as a distinct issue, access to safe and legal abortion as a distinct issue, and so on. Each of those, of course, is an important piece of our overall goal of full equality.

I think the same could be said when you look at the social justice movement, whether we're talking about reforms that need to be made in the criminal justice arena, whether we're talking about making sure that we're providing legal protections against discrimination for people who are part of the LGBTQ community. Each of these pieces is an important part of an overall goal of equality, and we have to understand that they intersect, and that when we fight for one, we are fighting for a goal that benefits all. Where we can find ways to intersect and support each other, we're going to do a better job of advancing that big goal and not just the separate little pieces and parts of it."

KAYLA BRIËT, Filmmaker, Composer, and Musician

"I was familiar with the term *intersectionality*, but what I didn't realize is that my whole life experience revolved around intersectionality—like, 'Whoa, that's the word to describe it.' I grew up with a multicultural background—my mom is Chinese and Dutch-Indonesian, my dad is full-blooded Native American. I grew up going to powwows and traditional dancing, Native American style. I also grew up folding dumplings and celebrating Chinese New Year. And there was this really confusing experience where I never knew exactly where I fit in, because I was a part of all these communities, but I never felt like I belonged to any specific community. In order to create my own story, I had to connect the dots between all of those different inspirations and infuse them into my own stories, and rediscover that. That was my experience with intersectionality: connecting the dots between many different communities and finding your own ground amongst all of that."

GABRIELLE GORMAN, Filmmaker and YoungArts Winner

"I think intersectionality is understanding the parts of your identity that could be privileged [and] the parts of your identity that are not. As a black woman, I am oppressed in that way. I also have a citizenship to America, which is something that a lot of people do not have and a lot of people really want. That gives me a lot of privilege. I don't have to worry about people misgendering me, and therefore I don't have to worry about people discriminating against me because of that. In [the] feminist [movement], you have to realize that women are oppressed in different ways depending on citizenship, race, sexuality, et cetera."

SARAH McBRIDE, National Press Secretary for the Human Rights Campaign and LGBTQ Activist

"No one is walking through this world or navigating this world with only one identity. We're all walking through this world with, frankly, an infinite number of identities, some of which give us privilege and some of which are marginalized. [Intersectionality] is an understanding of that multitude of identities in every person. For me, it's important to ingrain that in my work because if in my advocacy on LGBTQ equality I'm not also working on issues of racial justice, or immigrant rights, or gender equity, or combating xenophobia and Islamophobia, then I'm only gonna create change for the most privileged in my own community. I'm only gonna create change for those who maybe have one marginalized identity, but all of their other intersecting identities are identities of privilege. That's not the kind of change we need, and it's ignoring those who need it the most. So, I think being intersectional in your approach, it's not just necessary, it's the only way to go about change making."

AI-JEN POO, Director of the National Domestic Workers Alliance and Codirector of Caring Across Generations

"Intersectionality to me is about power. It's about how we come together from the place where our stories meet and how we build movements and campaigns, and how we essentially build power from the places where our interests intersect and come together. So if you're somebody who cares about the future of American families, I believe that that includes immigration reform and making sure that immigrant families can stay together because they're so much a part of the fabric of American family life. It's about how we tell stories that knit people together, and help people see their common interest and the way that their futures and their dreams are knitted together."

WAZINA ZONDON, Cocreator of *Coming Out Muslim: Radical Acts of Love*
"To me intersectionality means being willing to recognize that there are multiple ways and lenses through which one experience can be lived and received. Those lenses include race, geographic location, sexual orientation, faith, language—that kind of thing. And for me intersectionality impacts me at the core of my work, it reflects the primary form or method through which I have to approach anything that I do. Initially I came into this experience of intersectionality—[at least] the words of it—because I kept realizing that when I talked about gender or sexual orientation or whatever it was in college, and as a sex educator, my perspectives and the perspectives of the people who kind of looked like me or sounded like me were absent. And now intersectionality is also what I have to keep in mind when I do my work, because my students come in with a whole other range of ways that they are experiencing my classroom."

BOB BLAND, Women's March National Cochair
"We can't be activists and organizers only to the areas of our self-interests. That's really the heart of intersectionality, to take an issue that does not directly affect you and see yourself in that. Lift this other human being, who you may know or you may not know. And know that there will be no justice for you, for your children, for your family, for your community, until there's justice for all people, and all women."

JAMIA WILSON, Executive Director and Publisher of the Feminist Press at City University of New York

"Intersectionality is really about understanding the pillars of oppression in the world that impact our lives based on the various identities that we hold. So, when I think of systems of oppression that impact me, there's ableism because I was born with a visual disability, antiblack racism because I'm African American, and sexism because I am a cisgender woman. But I also have privileges that make it so that I get benefits that I was born into as well. So, I was born into an upper-middle-class family, I was able to access elite education, I've always had health insurance or it was somewhere within my grasp. And so those are the kinds of things, too, that when we show up with our identity, we're showing up with either the detriments that these systems have thrust upon us or the advantages that have helped us get where we are that have nothing to do with our merits or our own individual talent."

TINA TCHEN, Former Chief of Staff to First Lady Michelle Obama and Executive Director of the Obama White House Council on Women and Girls

"The issues that we have at hand—immigration reform, education reform, criminal justice reform, reproductive justice—each of those is impossible to understand in full without an intersectional lens. We have systems in place that historically and continuously create disadvantage for certain groups, and we can't fully appreciate the extent of that without looking at the cross section of identity. In this work, intersectionality means a deepened layer when we talk about diversity and inclusion. It means more than just having more women or more people of color at the table or in government. It means having more women of color, more immigrant women with disabilities, more LGBTQ women from low-income areas, just to name a few. That's intersectionality. And when we don't take on that lens, someone will get left behind."

ASHLEY JUDD, Actor, Author, and Activist

"*Ally* is a verb as well as a noun, so I need to approach folks who are different from me with an open mind and say, 'I need your help, please teach me about your experience.' Being an ally requires a constant self-scrutiny for humility. Admitting my lapses is important. My Papaw Judd used to say assuming makes an A-S-S out of you and me. Intersectionality means, to me, that so many factors are at play in creating the lived experience of every individual, including social, economic, educational, ethnic, and racial access to resources or lack thereof, and the type of political system in which one has been raised or is living."

ALICIA GARZA, Cofounder of Black Lives Matter Network and Special Projects Director at the National Domestic Workers Alliance

"Intersectionality looks at the ways in which race, class, gender, and other social positions impact our lived experiences. I see a lot of people talking about intersectionality these days, but they haven't taken the time to understand what it means and how it shows up in our lives. Intersectionality isn't diversity— it is fundamentally about relationships of power and how we embody those relationships, and the impacts that power has on our lives and on the lives of others. I encourage everyone to actually read Dr. Kimberlé Crenshaw's essay on intersectionality. We owe it to ourselves to get it right and not cut corners."

CHAPTER 5

○ ○ ○ ○ ○ ○ ○

YOUR STORY MATTERS
(AND OTHER THINGS THAT SOUND TRITE BUT ARE TRUE)

I'm an anxious person.

When I first sought treatment for my very official generalized anxiety disorder, the clinical diagnosis I was given in 2010 after going to see my very first New York City therapist, I was hesitant to talk about it. Even though I wasn't ashamed of getting help—I live in New York! It feels like everyone's in therapy!—there's still a certain taboo to admitting that you can't handle everything on your own. It's a weird and persistent double standard in our culture: going to the doctor to deal with a physical ailment? Totally normal. Going to a medical professional to deal with your mind? Still less normal.

And I was determined not to end up labeled the crazy girl. No one wants to be seen as crazy, and it's doubly bad to be the crazy *girl*.

As months in therapy turned to years, I became more open about the whole process. I quickly found out I wasn't alone.

I had to leave work early on Tuesdays to make my appointment, so I nervously told my boss. Her response? "Of course, I'm in therapy too! Do what you need to do." I started talking about it more with my friends, old and new. I ended up inundated with requests for therapist referrals. I realized that other people related to my story and wanted to talk about the way mental health issues impacted their lives too. And eventually, since I was working as a writer and editor at HuffPost, I decided to write about anxiety—including my own.

This felt particularly scary. If you're a woman with a point of view on the Internet, people are going to react strongly to you, often negatively so. And discussing something as personal as mental health brings an inevitable side of mocking, vitriol, armchair diagnosis, and dismissal. But when I published my first piece on women and anxiety, I was pleasantly surprised to discover that the response wasn't just Twitter trolls telling me that I'm a crazy bitch. In fact, many readers echoed relief that someone was articulating feelings that were deeply familiar.

The messages poured in: "Thank you so much for writing this!" "I forwarded your article to my boyfriend and said he had to read it if he wanted to understand me." "I relate to this so hard."

Sharing some of my personal struggles and experiences on a public platform—even in a small way—gave me a taste of how much our stories can impact the people we share them with.

I'm probably not the first person to tell you: "Your story matters." If you hear it enough, it begins to sound both painfully obvious and almost meaningless. If you're a millennial or a gen Z-er, you know all about storytelling—we do it regularly on social media. But as I began speaking with women for this book, the theme came up over and over and over again.

☆　☆　☆

YOUR STORY MATTERS

The way we think about our lives, our families, our nation, and our future relies on storytelling. We need to tell ourselves a story about our purpose and place in history and ascribe meaning to what we get up and do each day. If stories can guide our daily lives and tell us what it means to be an American, changing those things requires new and varied stories. And right now—though the landscape is changing—the stories that we hear most often and most loudly are still by and for and about able-bodied, straight, cisgender white men. If you fall outside of these labels—or within them but challenge the dominant narrative attached to those labels—telling your story and your truth can be a radical act.

"It's our responsibility to share our stories," nineteen-year-old filmmaker Kayla Briët told me, "because when we don't have our stories told, we become denied identity. And once we're denied identity, we become invisible. All of us human beings, we're all storytellers."

When you share your story, you tell the world that you deserve to be seen and heard. And when you share your story with someone who isn't exactly like you, you give them the gift of expanding their own world.

Ultimately, storytelling is a way to both create connections and assert the right to take up space, within your own community and with people outside of that community. And that's exactly what Wazina Zondon and Terna Tilley-Gyado's storytelling performance *Coming Out Muslim: Radical Acts of Love*[1] seeks to do in exploring the intersection of Muslim identity and queer identity.

"Coming Out Muslim" was first developed as an eight-week training for youth workers focused on disrupting Islamophobia ahead of the ten-year anniversary of 9/11. Zondon and Tilley-Gyado both identify as queer and Muslim, so it felt natural and important to them to include queer Muslim experiences and narratives within the training. Eventually, they were approached by one of the training participants, a theater major. She asked if they would be interested in continuing the conversation about queer Muslim experiences by developing a show. Zondon and Tilley-Gyado said yes. Thus, *Coming Out Muslim* was born.

"For both Terna and myself, we felt very invisible most of the time," Zondon told me. "We recognized the need and necessity to reclaim the narrative about who we are—as immigrants, as women, as Muslims, as women of color. And I think for young women, first-generation women, women of color, or queer girls, many of us don't have role models or path makers before us. And so this was an opportunity for us to make paths for the girls that will come after us."

Zondon compares storytelling to lobbying in its power to affect social change.

"Lobbying really at its source is telling the story that will get lawmakers to change their perspective," she explained. "And when you tell stories and you share your experiences and you hear other people's stories, you get to connect on the level of the heart."

There's some scientific evidence to back up the theory that exposure to someone's story—especially when it happens in an intimate setting among people who already know or identify with one another—can make an impact.[2] A 2006 review of 515 relevant studies found that "intergroup contact typically reduces intergroup prejudice."[3] In other words, that means that spending time around someone who is a member of a marginalized group that you are not a part of can decrease your biases and misconceptions about that group.

Of course, turning these heartening findings and anecdotal successes into a larger movement is not without its challenges. After all, a friend or family member opening up to another friend about her sexuality or her abortion or the racial discrimination she's experienced is likely to be far more effective when it comes to changing hearts and minds than a stranger watching another stranger's story on YouTube. (Look no further than the comments under any YouTube video for proof of that.)

Over the last five years, the abortion rights movement has particularly embraced storytelling as a tool for reducing stigma. The 1 in 3 Campaign,[4] which harnesses women's abortion stories to "begin to build a culture of compassion, empathy, and support for access to basic health care," and the Shout Your Abortion movement,[5] which started as a hashtag in 2015, are predicated on the idea that our stories contain untapped power.

Sometimes stories trickle out, one by one. Other times they burst forth, flooding and changing the landscape before we've had a moment to breathe. After the election of an alleged sexual predator, women tapped into their rage, accumulated over years of casual mistreatment and objectification and harassment (and in some cases sexual aggression and violence) at the hands of powerful men. They started telling their stories to journalists like Jodi Kantor, Megan Twohey, and Ronan Farrow. They declared "me too," a phrase coined by activist Tarana Burke and signal-boosted by actress Alyssa Milano. Twitter and Facebook and Instagram feeds were filled with stories of abuse and violation, stories that had been carefully buried, sometimes for decades. Me too. Her too. Them too. Us too.

The public largely believed the women and men and gender-nonconforming people telling these stories. Predatory men across industries lost their jobs. Women spoke up and the culture took notice. We will be sorting through the consequences of this reckoning for years to come. And although the jury is still out on how effective these campaigns are, it's worth remembering that social change takes time—lots of it. If our stories impact even just one person in a profound way, it's worth telling them.

☆   ☆   ☆

Sarah McBride understands intimately what a crucial role storytelling can play in advocacy. The twenty-seven-year-old LGBTQ activist boasts an insanely impressive résumé: not only is she the national press secretary for the Human Rights Campaign, but in 2016 she also became the first transgender American to address a major party convention when she spoke at the Democratic National Convention.

During that speech Sarah didn't simply speak about trans rights in generalities. She spoke about coming out while serving as student-body president at American University. And she spoke about her late husband and fellow LGBTQ activist, Andy Cray.[6] Sarah and Andy met in June 2012 at a White House reception honoring the LGBTQ community.[7] In 2013, Andy discovered that he had cancer, and in 2014, after a period of remission, that cancer came back. This time it was terminal. Sarah became a caregiver, and then she became a wife. She also became an even fiercer advocate for social change. It's this experience that she spoke about at the DNC.

"I met Andy, who was a transgender man, fighting for equality, and we fell in love," she told the thousands in the audience and the many more watching from home. "And yet even in the face of his terminal illness, this twenty-eight-year-old, he never wavered in his commitment to our cause

and his belief that this country can change. We married in 2014, and just four days after our wedding, he passed away."

Sarah used her own story to connect on a human level with those listening to her, and used that human connection to draw attention not only to her personal experience but to all of the far-reaching, intersectional work that still needs to be done when it comes to trans rights. And as she later explained to me, she believes that her ability to be a storyteller is what ultimately allowed her to advocate for the trans community at a national political party convention.

"Advocacy can't just be spouting off statistics. Advocacy has to come from the heart, and in many cases that includes storytelling," Sarah told me. "I had a story that I was willing to share that underscored the fact that transgender people are people—that transgender people love and hope and dream and fear and cry and laugh just like everyone else. It was important to all of us that with that platform, that short time onstage, we conveyed that simple fact to people who were watching. Because at the end of the day, there's the cliché 'People don't remember what you say, they remember how you make them feel.' And I was willing to share my personal story and stand on that stage and be, for lack of a better term, vulnerable in front of a lot of people. It's a lesson that I've learned over the course of my advocacy: sometimes the best path to power and equality is through public vulnerability and allowing people to see us in our full humanity."

That's a lesson that can be hard to take to heart—especially for women, who are socialized to believe that we should never put ourselves at the center. We think we might take up too much space, be too much. And while sometimes it's important to step aside, it's also on us to fight against these instincts to an extent that we don't end up invisible and unheard. We need to tell our own stories and use whatever privilege we have to amplify the stories of others. We need to assert that we matter. You. Matter.

Senator Elizabeth Warren said it best, when I asked her why we needed young women's voices in the fight for social justice.

"Young women have valuable experiences and perspectives," she said. "They will enrich the political discussion and help us reach more inclusive decisions. I look at it this way—if you don't have a seat at the table, then you're probably on the menu."

Part Two

HOW TO
RESIST LIKE A GIRL

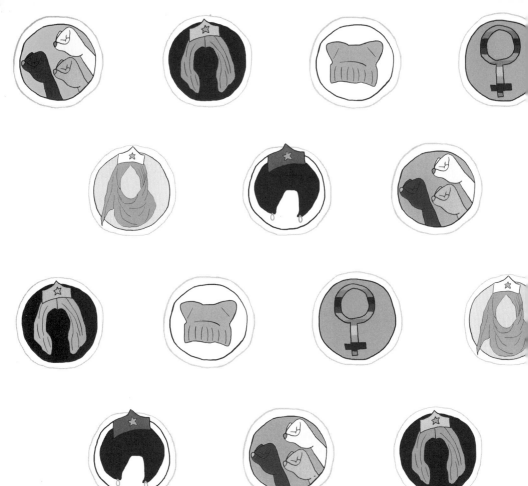

CHAPTER 6

○ ○ ○ ○ ○ ○ ○

HOW TO STOP WATCHING
NETFLIX, GET OFF YOUR COUCH, AND
GET SH*T DONE NOW

We have to do *something*."

This sentence played through my head thousands of times on November 9, 2016.

I had been dragged into the HuffPost office that morning by my work wife, Jess, on about three and a half hours of restless sleep. The night before, my team and I had left the Javits Center (the glass-ceilinged building where Hillary Clinton's election night watch party was taking place) after one of us broke out in hives, one of us broke out in a heat rash, and one of us (read: me) found herself on her knees outside trying to stave off a panic attack as one of her favorite actresses chain-smoked mere feet away.

We ended up around the corner from Javits and spent the remainder of the night into the early-morning hours speaking to the men and women who were leaving Clinton's public block party. They streamed out in groups, clutching one another and the American flags that had been given out during a more hopeful hour, some rolled up tightly and some gripped in fists. We were all just trying to hold on.

I gave up on even that base-level goal around 1:30 A.M. My credit card refused to work as I tried to pay for my taxi ride back to Brooklyn. I was exhausted after a long, unexpected night's work. My heart hurt—I was grief-stricken, and in that moment it felt like someone had died. More than that, it felt like my country—or at least the tenuous, idealized vision I had of it—had died. As I swiped my card for the fifth and then sixth time, I broke. I burst into ragged sobs, to the point where the poor driver had to pull over and help me work the credit card machine.

"I'm scared too," he told me as he helped me out of the taxi and onto the curb outside my apartment.

The next day felt like a blur—partly because I had eventually taken a sleeping pill to force myself to get a bit of shut-eye, and partly because it seemed like everyone I knew, regardless of political worldview, was trying to figure out what came next. We would not have our first woman president. We would instead have a president who had campaigned on an openly anti-immigrant, anti-Muslim, anti-woman platform.

I wrote like a motherfucker (as Cheryl Strayed would say) that day, because work has always helped me process my most ragged emotions. By the afternoon I was gripped by an overwhelming need to do more.

"In dire need of the wonderful women in my life. Feeling thankful they exist," I emailed my friend Lindsey.

She responded quickly with a post-work plan: "Let's go somewhere dark. Quiet. And where it's always four A.M."

And so we did just that, recruiting Jess and our friend Julie to come along. Out of that night of brainstorming came a mission. We were going to create a space for empowerment and action on a day when many Americans would need it: Inauguration Day.

☆   ☆   ☆

While I was desperately trying not to throw up (and trying to write a story) in a giant, fluorescent-lit room at the Javits Center, thirty-three-year-old Haley Stevens was upstairs trying to maintain a sense of what she termed "optimistic denial."

Haley, who worked for Hillary Clinton's 2008 presidential campaign and subsequently took a post in the Obama administration, flew into New York City from southeastern Michigan to attend what she assumed would be Clinton's victory party with one of her best friends from college. Instead, she wound up in a crowded room trying to be upbeat while she fielded texts from friends and family all over the country and watched Clinton supporters and staffers burst into tears.

She stayed at the Javits Center until the wee hours, when Clinton's campaign chairman, John Podesta, finally came out and announced that Clinton would not be addressing her supporters that night. As someone who had volunteered extensively for the campaign and knew many of Clinton's staffers, Haley ended up going out with them until six in the morning, cracking jokes and trying to keep everyone's energy up. And she found herself saying out loud that she might run for office.

"At the election night party I was hyped, because I was really furious," she told me. "I remember saying, 'I think I might run for something. I might run.' I just was like, 'The only way I can respond to this is by stepping up.'"

So she stepped up. Haley began fund-raising for a congressional run in Michigan's Eleventh District, located just northwest of Detroit, encompassing parts of Wayne and Oakland Counties. She hopes to channel her anger and energy into making a difference in her home state, a place she knows and cares about deeply.

And Haley is far from alone.

Hillary Clinton's loss, and the rise of Donald Trump—a political figure so diametrically opposed to Clinton and women's rights as a whole—motivated *thousands* of women to consider elected office.

Within a month after the election, She Should Run, a nonpartisan organization dedicated to "expanding the talent pool of future elected female leaders," heard from more than forty-five hundred women across the political spectrum.[1] By mid-February, that number had risen to nearly thirteen thousand.

She Should Run founder and CEO Erin Loos Cutraro summed up what she was seeing in the months following Trump's election and inauguration: "There's an air of activism right now—and it's having a snowball effect."

Rachel Thomas, former communications director at EMILY's List, a political action committee (PAC) that works to elect pro-choice Democratic women across the nation, called the drive of women to run for office since President Trump took office "unprecedented."

By mid-April 2017, EMILY's List had heard from more than eleven thousand women.[2] In the previous twenty-two months, they'd heard from nine hundred.

"Women run for office because they want to fix something or they're mad as hell about something," said Rachel. "And [the presidential] election brought out women who might feel one way, or might feel both ways, about what they're seeing in Washington and their state legislatures across the country."

Being "mad as hell" can be a great tool for motivating yourself to do that fixing. And that's because anger—righteous, energizing, directed anger—is a powerful force.

☆　☆　☆

But, of course, it can't end at anger. That anger needs to translate into action.

My post-election anger, coupled with the post-election anger of a handful of other women, turned into a summit on January 21, 2017. Through our event Watch Us Run, my friends (who also happen to be my colleagues) and I turned manic energy and fear into something light and tangible.

Of course, before Watch Us Run could be an actual thing, we had to do a hell of a lot of work. My co-organizers and I were lucky enough to work for name-brand media companies, which meant we had platforms and a decent base of contacts, but none of us had ever planned a summit from the ground up. (The biggest event I had planned prior to this one was probably a staff trip for my summer camp. So I basically had no clue what I was doing.)

Our goals were simple: attract interesting speakers from either side of the political aisle, figure out a venue in a location that would make sense for an event being held on Inauguration Day, promote the event to attract enough people to attend, and somehow fund the whole thing. Okay, so not actually simple at all.

My friends and I started by going back to our bosses and their bosses and asking if HuffPost and Bustle would be willing to put their names behind our event. We brought in more of our colleagues—women in leadership positions at both brands across editorial, communications, and marketing. We decided we would be scrappy, and that we weren't above begging for money to get this thing off the ground. A consultant for Bustle happened to be a member of the National Press Club, and by some small miracle they still had rooms available for rent on Inauguration Day. The space was affordable and downtown in Washington, DC, so we jumped at the chance to secure it, assuming we'd figure out the rest as we went.

And somehow we did!

We sent emails to every high-profile, politically engaged woman we had contact information for. We crafted pitches for marketing purposes. We reached out to feminist brands that might be interested in donating merchandise for the gift bags we gave our speakers, all of whom agreed to participate for free. We planned a run of the show, centered on the themes of grassroots activism, art as resistance, and running for elected office. HuffPost's parent company, AOL, was kind enough to assign someone on the events team to help us figure out logistics with the venue. (Her name is Sara, and we referred to her as "literal angel" for that whole month. She performed miracles, such as getting costs shaved down so that we didn't blow through our meager budget and saving us from having the event in a room with very little airflow and far too much backlighting.)

It all began to feel very real when Jess, HuffPost's then director of communications, Lena, and I wound up on a phone call with Ashley Judd, actress and activist extraordinaire. Despite being under the weather, Ashley was interested in being a keynote speaker at our summit. And unlike many celebrities who only communicate through their publicists, she wanted to be on the phone with us to really talk through her involvement. After we hung up the phone, the three of us did a silent happy dance in a huddle room. Maybe this thing would actually make some sort of small impact after all.

The day before Donald Trump was sworn in as president of the United States, five of us spent hours doing a walk-through of the event space for Watch Us Run, reviewing logistics and stuffing gift bags in a tiny hallway. It was tedious work, but it was also invigorating. We were creating something—in the place where they would be holding the #MAGA DeploraBall that night, no less—and we were working rather than wallowing. It felt damn good.

On Inauguration Day, 400 men and women packed into the National Press Club in DC. We had panels on how to run for office, the role of art in resistance, and grassroots activism. Michael Moore led us in a group primal scream, and Ashley Judd and Representative Barbara Lee led affirmations.

We streamed all of it on Facebook Live, and 1.5 million people across the country tuned in.

"I will feel all my feelings," said Ashley Judd, wearing a pink pussy hat, as the audience repeated her words back to her.

After the day wrapped up, a man I had never met approached me. Lindsey and I had been emceeing the event, so we had hardly paused to speak to anyone.

"Thank you," he told me earnestly as he gave me a warm hug. "You saved my day."

Our small summit wouldn't change the world or the country, but it did change a few people's days. And that was a start.

Like me and like Haley, so many women across the country—and the world—felt compelled in the wake of a confusing and divisive election to do more. And if you're reading this book, you probably want to do more too.

☆   ☆   ☆

SIMPLE WAYS TO JOIN THE RESISTANCE TODAY (OR TOMORROW, BECAUSE SOMETIMES TODAY IS REALLY FREAKING EXHAUSTING)

1. CALL, FAX, EMAIL, AND CONFRONT YOUR REPS. Set an alarm on your phone, find a buddy to hold you accountable, and just do it. Be reasonable about the commitment—can you find ten minutes every day? Every other day? Make a plan and stick to it. When your senator

or congressperson has a town hall, show up. If they haven't scheduled a town hall, ask them to. When people express their concerns in large numbers, our elected representatives have to listen.

2. RUN FOR OFFICE—AND/OR ENCOURAGE THE WOMEN IN YOUR LIFE TO. Okay, so this one isn't exactly simple, and you don't have to do it right away, but it's deeply important. The more women who run for office, the more women who win. And the more women who win, the more seats at the table we have.

If you're interested in exploring a run for office at some point in the future, get in touch with organizations such as She Should Run, EMILY's List, Run for Something, Ignite, Sister District, and Emerge. And if there's a woman you know who you think would make a great candidate, nominate her through She Should Run's Ask a Woman to Run for Office program.

3. DONATE WHAT YOU CAN. There are already organizations out there that are dedicated to nearly any cause you can think of. And the number one thing most of them need right now? Money. It may sound unglamorous or lazy, but truly, these groups—most of whom have been doing this work for years—need to pay their employees, purchase materials, and keep their doors open. Your donations, no matter how small, can make a difference. For more info on this, go to page 112.

4. VOLUNTEER YOUR TIME. As Mother of the Movement Lucy McBath told me: "Start volunteering your time and your effort. That's how you grow into an activist or a movement. That's all it simply is, is that being mad enough and angry enough about something to make a difference."

5. START HAVING TOUGH CONVERSATIONS WITH PEOPLE YOU MIGHT DISAGREE WITH—OFFLINE. Absolutely *don't* get on Twitter and start spamming your trolls with links to op-eds about health care and immigration—or tweets that cleverly tell them to fuck off. Not only is that unfulfilling (except maybe in the moment), but it's a waste of time and emotional energy. What you absolutely *should* do is start wading into loving, empathetic chats with friends and family members who come at a given issue from a different vantage point than you do.

"One of the negative effects of social media is that we don't have the deep recurring conversations that we need to have to move people forward in their awareness and in their empathy and in their shared humanity," Women's March national cochair Bob Bland told me. "Twitter is the most political [social media platform], and it's also the most cutthroat platform, because it allows you the shortest amount of time to make a statement. And so in one hundred forty characters you're going to condense whatever it is you're trying to express into the most potent statement you can. That can be beautiful if it's love, but all too often it's hate or fear or cynicism."

She also pointed out the obvious: that people speak to one another very differently on Twitter or Facebook or Snapchat than they do in real life. To encourage people to talk face-to-face with people they already know, the Women's March organizers launched an initiative called Daring Discussions,[3] along with a tool kit to help you start such conversations, which can be found at daringdiscussions.com. The tool kit includes guidelines—"ground yourself in love," "be aware of the privilege you hold," "be unconditionally accepting"—as well as sample questions: "What motivated you to participate in this discussion?" "What are you most hopeful about when you think about the future?" "What do you want to know but have been afraid to ask about the other side of this topic?"

These empathetic conversations only work when both people involved are open to having them. Don't go in looking to definitively change anyone's mind. Go in looking for understanding. You may end up finding common ground you never knew existed.

6. LISTEN TO THE WOMEN WHO ARE ALREADY LEADING THE RESISTANCE, ESPECIALLY WOMEN OF COLOR. There's an instinct among a lot of young women to want to start something when they experience a political awakening. And it's understandable—you want to be as involved as possible! You want to feel ownership over this energy and the impact you'd like to make! But there are veterans in the

trenches who have been fighting this fight for years—seek them out and follow them because they will know where your energy would be best applied.

Toward the end of November I accompanied my friend Liz to an organizing meeting at an acquaintance's Brooklyn townhouse. There were activists of all different areas of expertise and backgrounds in attendance. But something that really struck me was when a young black woman stood up and addressed her white sisters in the room. She asked us to put ourselves on the front lines of the resistance so that women of color didn't always have to be there, standing alone.

7. SHOW UP, SHOW UP, SHOW UP—EVEN WHEN IT'S NOT DIRECTLY ABOUT YOU. Your body is your greatest tool and weapon. Deploy it wisely, to physically be there for the people and causes you care about. If you're a white woman, this is doubly important.

We all tend to get the most fired up when our personal rights are impacted. After all, empathy takes work. But the fight for human rights is ultimately one fight. If we leave people to fend only for themselves, we will all ultimately fail.

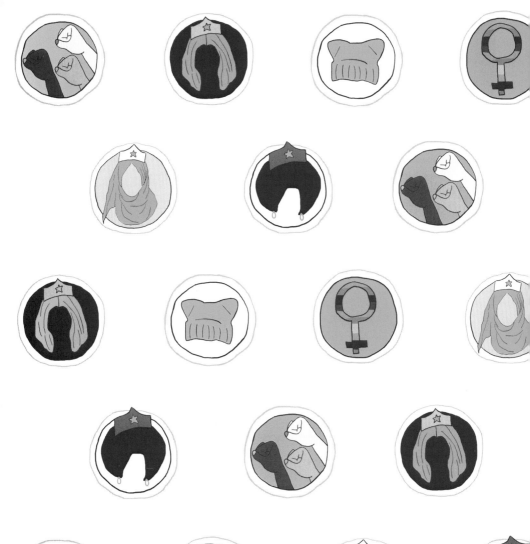

CHAPTER 7

○ ○ ○ ○ ○ ○ ○

A TECH-SAVVY GUIDE TO
STAYING ACCOUNTABLE

So . . . you're angry, you're motivated, and you want to make a difference. But what comes next? It's easy to feel as though you're getting swept up in a Twitter/Facebook/news spiral that leaves you with a whole lot of anxiety and very little idea of what to do about it. Luckily, we have it much easier than the women who came before us, because many of us are walking around with tiny computers in our hands at all times. Thanks to smartphones, data, and readily accessible Wi-Fi, it's easier than ever to access our elected representatives basically anytime, anywhere.

To get you started, here are some apps, websites, and guides that can help direct your activism, keep you on track, and make sure you're using the time you have to dedicate to the cause wisely. You can fax your senator via text, donate funds to fight for women's rights and criminal justice reform with a few taps, and get (a gif of) Beyoncé delivered into your inbox along with a call to action.

What a time to be alive.

If you want to text your reps...

USE: **RESISTBOT**

WHAT IT IS: A bot that lets you send official-looking faxes to your senators and congresspersons, all through text message.

HOW IT WORKS: To get started, text "RESIST" to 50409. The bot will prompt you to give your name and address in order to locate your representatives. Once you've done that, you just type the message you want to send to your reps and text that to the bot. Resistbot does the rest of the work for you, putting together an official-looking fax, complete with your address, your representative's DC office address, the date, and a signature. You even get a follow-up text confirming that the fax has been received.

WHY IT'S GREAT: You're not reading off a script or copy-pasting someone else's talking points. You can really personalize your messages, but because it's over text, it just feels easier than sitting down and crafting an email. And if something pisses you off while you're out with friends or doing work or trying to come up with that truly perfect 140-character zinger, within five minutes you can let your senator know exactly how you feel.

If you want your action to come with a side of comprehensive information...

USE: **COUNTABLE**

WHAT IT IS: An app (which is also available as a website) that keeps you up to date on political news and upcoming local and national legislation—and lets you contact your representatives directly from articles.

HOW IT WORKS: Countable has several moving parts. The core of the app is a running list of bills that will be voted on in Congress. When users tap into a bill, Countable provides a summary and details of the legislation, a "yea" argument, a "nay" argument, an explanation of how far the legislation has progressed, and the ability to vote on said legislation. These yea or nay votes are then tallied and sent along to your representatives. The app also has a news feed that gives neutral updates on and explanations of political news. Users can comment on specific bills or news within the app and have the option to call or message their reps directly from articles.

WHY IT'S GREAT: Countable has it all—unbiased explanations of legislation, easy ways to take action and share information, and a simple way to keep up with all the things your representatives are voting on. You can even register to vote through Countable and get email alerts when your reps cast votes!

If you want to turn the country blue . . .

USE: SWING LEFT

WHAT IT IS: A mailing list that sends its members curated calls to action, based on the swing district closest to where they live. Swing Left's goal is to help Democrats take back a majority in the House.

HOW IT WORKS: You go to swingleft.org and type in your address or zip code. Swing Left then determines where the closest "swing" district—that is, a district that Democrats may have a chance of winning or won narrowly in the previous election—is. You can then sign up to join the "team" helping in that district. Once you do that, Swing Left will send you emails (but not so frequently that they will overwhelm your inbox) with ways to get involved: fund-raising, knocking on doors for a specific candidate, registering voters, phone banking, events, and more.

WHY IT'S GREAT: If you are someone who wants to be involved in progressive electoral politics but lives in a solidly blue district, Swing Left gives you tangible ways to help.

If you want to put your money where your mouth is . . .

USE: **SUPER GOOD**

WHAT IT IS: A platform that lets you make daily donations to organizations that support the causes you care about.

HOW IT WORKS: You can create a profile on super-good.org through your Gmail, Facebook, or Twitter account. Once you've signed up, you can choose causes to support and choose an amount of money to donate per day. Your daily donation is multiplied by thirty, and that amount is charged to your credit card on a monthly basis. Super Good then handles splitting up your donations among the causes you've selected and donating the total funds to each organization they support on a monthly basis. Super Good focuses on ten major causes: free press, education, environment, civil liberties, women's rights, anti-hate, criminal justice reform, immigration, indigenous rights, and LGBTQ rights. The funds that Super Good collects for each cause are distributed among three different organizations per cause—for example, Planned Parenthood, Black Lives Matter, the Southern Poverty Law Center, and Earthjustice. According to Super Good's website, the causes and organizations will evolve over time.

WHY IT'S GREAT: It can be super overwhelming to feel like you can't afford to donate to all of the causes that matter. Through Super Good, you don't have to choose between fighting police brutality and fighting climate change, and you don't have to set up fifteen different recurring donations. And since you can donate as little as fifty cents per day, it all feels financially manageable.

If you want something to do every day . . .

USE: **DAILY ACTION**

WHAT IT IS: A text bot that sends you a call to action each weekday and connects you directly to your representatives.

HOW IT WORKS: To get started, you text "DAILY" to 228466. You will then be prompted for your zip code. Once that's all done, Daily Action will text you each morning with something to do. Past calls to action have focused on things like calling members of Congress to demand that stronger economic sanctions be imposed against Russia, joining the Women's March, and urging representatives to oppose the Trump administration's health care bill. The bot also connects you directly to your reps with a quick swipe.

WHY IT'S GREAT: Calling your representatives is considered one of the most effective ways to get their attention—after all, often a staffer has to physically pick up the phone. Daily Action makes that call easy and routine. During the first week of Donald Trump's presidency alone, more than ten thousand people made calls to Congress through Daily Action.

If you're phone-shy . . .

USE: **5 CALLS**

WHAT IT IS: An app (which is also available as a website) that guides you through five calls to your representatives each day, depending on what's important to you.

HOW IT WORKS: Download the app or go to 5calls.org and type in your location. You will be asked what's important to you that day, from a list of ten options. These choices change depending on where you live, what legislation is upcoming, and what's going on in the news. Once you choose, 5 Calls will direct you to a summary of an issue and provide you with a fill-in-the-blanks script to guide calls to your representatives. You can call your congressperson and senators right from the app, and after you call, the app lets you log the outcome: Did you make contact? Leave a voicemail? Was your rep unavailable? No matter what, log it and move on to call number two.

WHY IT'S GREAT: Sometimes it's just too exhausting or nerve-wracking to figure out what to say once you get someone from your representative's office on the phone—phone calls can be super awkward! And while it's ideal to personalize every call you make, having a script can be a huge relief.

If you need motivation to keep fighting . . .

USE: **SIGNAL BOOST**

WHAT IT IS: A kickass intersectional feminist online newsletter (and a weekly SiriusXM show!) dedicated to "boosting the hell out of the great work being done in the resistance," founded by former Hillary Clinton campaign staffers Zerlina Maxwell and Jess McIntosh.

HOW IT WORKS: Sign up and wait for the emails to arrive. Each one contains an update on a few key issues and suggestions for concrete ways to act on those issues. Think of it like theSkimm for the resistance (an archive of Signal Boost blasts can be found at signal-boost.com).

WHY IT'S GREAT: It's concise, women-led, and fun to read. Some weeks are harder than others, and when you get exhausted and feel like giving up, Zerlina and Jess are there to remind you to keep going. Plus, the gifs are excellent and often feature Beyoncé. #DoItForTheGifs

If you want to play the long game . . .

USE: **INDIVISIBLE**

WHAT IT IS: A comprehensive guide to resisting the Trump agenda using local actions, as laid out by former congressional staffers.

HOW IT WORKS: The guide grew out of a simple post-election question: For progressive America, what comes next? Two congressional staffers looked at the basic tactics of the Tea Party during the Obama years and used them as a framework to create a guide (originally put online in a Google Doc) for progressives who wanted to know how to resist. The guide also included information on how members of Congress think, and suggested the best ways to get under their skin and command their attention. Since then, Indivisible has grown into much more than a guide. Indivisible groups have popped up all over the nation, and the Indivisible website (indivisible.org) lets you find resources, locate local groups to join, and register your own group in the Indivisible network.

WHY IT'S GREAT: Indivisible isn't just a guide—it's a movement.

If you don't have easy access to a computer or smartphone . . .

USE: **THE LOCAL PUBLIC LIBRARY!** (or your school's computer lab, if you're in school)

WHAT IT IS: You already know this one.

HOW IT WORKS: Log on to a computer and go to usa.gov/elected-officials. This website will allow you to look up the senators, congressperson, and local elected officials who represent you, then figure out who it makes the most sense to contact. Are you worried about a bill that the House is considering? Call or email your representative. Do you want to make sure your city remains a sanctuary city or upholds the Paris Climate Accord? Call or email your mayor. Elected officials have their office's phone number and email address on their individual websites, and if you go to house.gov/representatives or senate.gov /senators/contact, you can find all the contact information for members of Congress in one place.

WHY IT'S GREAT: Because anyone can do it!

AND JUST SO YOU HAVE IT OFFLINE, HERE IS A VERY BASIC SCRIPT
TO HELP GUIDE YOUR CALLS AND EMAILS:

CALLING YOUR REP?

Hi, I'm a YOUR STATE/DISTRICT voter, and I'm calling to urge NAME OF ELECTED OFFICIAL to WHATEVER YOU WANT THEM TO DO.

As a YOUNG PERSON/WOMAN/PERSON OF COLOR/OTHER IDENTITY, this is deeply important to me and other voters like me. ADD ANY RELATED PERSONAL STORY, IF YOU HAVE ONE.

Thank you for your time.

EMAILING YOUR REP?

Hi, NAME OF ELECTED OFFICIAL,

My name is YOUR NAME, and I'm a voter in your STATE/DISTRICT. I'm writing to express YOUR FEELING about X ISSUE. INCLUDE ANY PERSONAL EXPERIENCE YOU'VE HAD WITH THE ISSUE HERE.

Thank you for taking the time to consider this, and I urge you to SUGGESTED ACTION.

Best,

YOUR NAME

CHAPTER 8

○ ○ ○ ○ ○ ○ ○

LADY CLUBS AND COVENS:
WHERE THE REAL WORK
(AND MAGIC) HAPPENS

Three days after the 2016 presidential election, a new friend slid into my Twitter DMs ... to invite me to a feminist consciousness-raising meeting.

"Hey lady," she wrote. "I'm not sure if someone forwarded you the message, but I'm having people over for a consciousness-raising meeting to discuss feelings and practical actions that we can take to ... you know, try to stop the human rights apocalypse."

I immediately accepted her invitation.

You might be asking: Emma, what the heck is a consciousness-raising meeting and why does it sound like something out of the 1960s and '70s? If the term sounds a bit retro, that's because it is—consciousness raising is an activist strategy popularized in the late sixties by radical leaders within the women's movement. The idea is pretty simple: come together, in person, to share life experiences with other women in order to understand what it actually means to be "oppressed" on a practical level. Saying sexism exists is one thing. Hearing five or ten or fifteen women discuss the overlapping ways that sexism plays out for *them* is quite another. Conclusions drawn in these groups can then be used to draft papers or spark actions.

Radical feminist Carol Hanisch—best known for popularizing the statement "the personal is political"[1]—wrote about the beginnings of consciousness raising within the women's movement for the feminist magazine *On the Issues* in 2010. According to Hanisch, during a 1968 New York Radical Women meeting, Anne Forer, another member of the group, said that women needed to "raise our consciousness" in order to properly consider themselves an oppressed group.

As Hanisch wrote of that meeting, "Anne went on to list a number of things women had to do to make themselves attractive to men, like not wearing our glasses, playing dumb, doing all kinds of painful things to our bodies, wearing uncomfortable clothing and shoes, going on diets—all because 'people don't find the real self of a woman attractive.'"

This naming of specific (and personal) forms of oppression, regardless of how seemingly small, was picked up by other members of the group, specifically Kathie Sarachild, who took the phrase and tactic and ran with it. Later that year Sarachild presented "A Program for Feminist Consciousness Raising" at the First National Women's Liberation Conference. By 1971, the concept was so popular that a pamphlet distributed by the Chicago Women's Liberation Union[2] began by stating definitively: "Consciousness-raising groups are the backbone of the Women's Liberation Movement."

Forty-eight years after Forer expressed the need to "raise our consciousness," I was invited to do the same, in the very same city.

The friend of mine who planned this meeting, Erin Darke, had just come off starring in *Good Girls Revolt*, an Amazon show that centered on women—specifically the women of a fictionalized version of *Newsweek*—getting "woke" to the need for women's liberation in 1969 into 1970.

The show was based on a true story. In 1970, forty-six female researchers at *Newsweek* sued the magazine for gender discrimination, because as women they were allowed to research and report stories but not actually write them. Both in real life and on the show, consciousness-raising meetings played a key role in getting enough women on board with filing an official complaint and in organizing plans for such a complaint. Preparing for and shooting the scenes that depicted this awakening had made a real impression on Erin.

"The consciousness-raising meeting scenes were some of my favorite scenes to shoot, and I just remember every time we would shoot one I'd just sit there being like, why don't we do this anymore?" Erin told me. "It was a huge part of what empowered so many women to know that they weren't alone. So I left the show thinking about that—and then the election happened."

Erin felt like Donald Trump's election was an attack on her humanity as a woman. So the next day she composed an email to the women in her life inviting them to a consciousness-raising meeting, like the ones she had acted out on *Good Girls Revolt*.

Three days later she headed down to DC for a *Good Girls Revolt*–related panel with Eleanor Holmes Norton—current congresswoman and the former ACLU lawyer who had helped organize the women of *Newsweek*.[3] Eleanor spoke about what feminism looked like in the sixties and seventies, and what she worried younger women might miss out on.

"She worried about our generation of women because we seemed to be so separated. It was like we had been trained to compete against each other for the success that we now knew was possible," remembered Erin. "As soon as she said that, I realized that was the thing I had been feeling and couldn't really put words to. I just deeply missed a sense of community among women."

Erin hoped that gathering some women in her living room might be a first step toward reclaiming that sense of community.

So, a week after getting Erin's message, I headed over to her apartment, not quite sure what I'd be walking into.

That first night I found myself in a room with about twenty other women and one woke dude. Very quickly, it became clear that although this space was not going to be totally exclusionary to men, its mission was going to be built around and led by women. That evening included a lot of feelings and a lot of tears and a lot of open-ended questions. Three hours later we knew that it would become something more.

Over the months that followed we continued to meet, and when a few people emailed Erin asking if they could bring boyfriends or straight male friends into the fold, she decided against it.

"The experience of being a woman is something that everyone in that room understands," Erin explained. "I do think that sense of common understanding is so powerful, and it has led to people being able to come and feel really comfortable and included immediately, and also to feel okay being vulnerable."

Another group member (and friend), Kate Dearing, told me that having a women-focused space helped create an atmosphere that was both emotionally intimate and primed for practical action.

"We have a bunch of highly functional, effective women that will just throw down. But at the same time, there is a kind of intimacy," she said. "People come and share stories and we do hug, and cheerlead, and emotionally support each other, and then we're also like, okay, how do we want to be engaged? How do we make a difference in this reality? And I think that combination is so powerful. So good for souls."

By mid-December the group had a name—Women to the Front—and by mid-July the group had raised more than fifteen thousand dollars for EMW Women's Surgical Center,[4] the very last abortion clinic in the state of Kentucky. The event was a resounding success. We raffled off Sam B. tickets and did sound checks and danced the night away. My friends, new and old, had created a space where people could gather and love one another and affirm their commitment to building a world where women's bodies are their own, where activism and joy can go hand in hand.

To tweak a beloved *Hamilton* quote: Women, we get the job done.

☆　　☆　　☆

Second-wave feminists (1960s) understood the value of creating spaces for and by women. Half a century later, those spaces are no less valuable.

They may look a little different in 2018 than in 1968, but the basic tenet of fostering shared experiences and understanding remains. The Internet—specifically social media—has offered endless opportunities for virtual connection. I am a part of three different feminist LISTSERVs, on which women are able to have near-daily debates, share information, and organize real-life meet-ups in various cities.

"We need spaces both on and offline where we can build and share ideas without interruption," said Jamia Wilson, former executive director of WAM! (Women, Action and the Media), the organization that runs one of those aforementioned feminist LISTSERVs. "And without mansplaining. And to be able to develop strength as a community and to create shared strategy passing."

Advocacy organizations such as WAM! have learned that the best way to activate existing members and reach new ones is—surprise!—online. Higher Heights, an organization dedicated to "building a national infrastructure to harness Black women's political power and leadership potential," often hosts Twitter-based Sunday brunches,[5] using the hashtags #BlackWomenLead and #SundayBrunch. These hashtags help facilitate discussions on topics such as running for office and what's at stake for black women under the Trump administration.

#BLACKWOMENLEAD
#SUNDAYBRUNCH 🥂

Many women I spoke to—both established activists and organizers and newly minted ones—expressed that in the wake of Trump's election they simply wanted to be around other women. So it only seemed natural to begin new organizing efforts with other women in mind.

Anna Poe-Kest, who lives in New York City and works in city government, spent much of November and December 2016 going to various politicalish meet-ups with women friends and colleagues. One such gathering was made up entirely of women who work in city government—a lot of "type A personalities," as Anna put it. These meet-ups felt cathartic at first, but after a while she began to feel as though there was a lot of talking going on but not a whole lot of productive, concrete action.

Then the Women's March happened.

Anna and a few of those same women, who also happen to be her close friends, knew they wanted to go down to DC. They decided to tap back into the group they had met up with weeks prior and head down to DC. "All of us still had it in our minds," said Anna. "We weren't ready to let it die."

They ended up renting a big van and piling about fifteen people into it. They also found housing in DC for every person who caravaned down with them. It was completely chaotic—and it felt great.

Reinvigorated from the march, Anna and her friends Elana Leopold, Monica Klein, and Ishanee Parikh reconvened in New York to really think through what they could do to resist on a long-term basis. Their first brainstorm session lasted six hours. They wanted to make sure that if they created something, it would fill an existing gap, rather than trying to replicate work that other people were already doing. So they spent time thinking about their unique skills and what they had access to that other young women who are otherwise like them might not.

"Part of it is that having grown up in this world, having had our first jobs in politics and New York City government, we've been able to make all these connections to these amazing women who are all of our mentors—the best, most sought-after communications specialists for campaigns or the second in command below the mayor, for example," said Anna. "At the same time we saw a lot of our friends, who maybe had never been in a courthouse before, or had never been to a mass protest before the Women's March, and they were so inspired by it but didn't really know how to do anything afterward. They were going to get fatigued and needed to figure out how to turn that into sustained activism that doesn't just die out. Protest is not the new brunch. It was for like a month, and it's not anymore."

And so out of those brainstorm sessions came the Broad Room. Its mission[6] is ambitious—to "train an army of young women in NYC to take political action and resist the right-wing agenda."

To build this nonviolent "army," the Broad Room does three things: (1) holds practical trainings on activism and government, led by experts, that is, the mentors of the organization's founders; (2) sends out a weekly newsletter, *The Broad Memo*, with practical calls to action; and (3) holds social events to foster connection between members—because what's activism without some levity and joy?

And (if you haven't already gathered) each of these three things is led by and for women. Anna told me that early on, the women of the Broad Room decided that they would be happy to have men donate their time and skill sets to behind-the-scenes work or to fund-raising, but any role at the center—whether as leadership or trainer or benefactor—would be taken up by women.

"If a man wants to do some pro bono design work for us, that we'll obviously give credit for, we will let him do that. And men can give us money and do all that shit. But anyone who's actually benefiting from our work is going to be a woman," said Anna. "So all the trainers are women. Any speaker at any of our events is a woman. We feature art in each of our *Broad Memo*s, and all of that is by women. Part of that decision I think came on a personal level—all of us working in politics, we're in very male-dominated spaces. And there's a totally different way that you act in a woman-dominated space as opposed to a space where there are men. 'Cause men often take over the room."

The advantages of having an activist space run by women go beyond women feeling empowered to speak up and lead. There are simply things— like motherhood—that are understood and considered more frequently and with greater care in such spaces. Women's March national cochair Bob Bland gave birth to her second daughter, Chloe, about ten days into march planning. After spending three days in the hospital, Bland was back out and organizing—with her newborn in tow. Coming from the fashion and startup worlds, she found working with her march cochairs a welcome contrast, like night and day. And Bland says that it never would have been possible for her to work as hard as she did leading up to the march if she hadn't been working with other women.

"I went straight back into organizing," she said. "And the only way I could do that was because [the Women's March] was women-led and because Tamika [Mallory] is a mother of her son, Tarique, and then Linda [Sarsour] has three children of her own, teenagers. And Carmen [Perez] has just so many nieces and nephews that she's helped to raise. [. . .] As much as we were working ourselves to the core every single day, harder than we'd ever worked in our lives, just knowing that it was okay for me to bring my child and that I didn't have to explain things was incredible. It was all right for me to breastfeed in public, and I wasn't gonna be asked to go sit over there."

Understanding that a new mom has to breastfeed seems simple, but it's something that even many modern workplaces still struggle with. Given both the recognition that women-led spaces are best equipped to address these "simple" needs and the reality that freelancers now make up more than one-third of the American workforce,[7] it's no wonder that work spaces that explicitly cater to women are having such a moment.

Women's co-working spaces[8] and social clubs such as the Wing (New York City), Hera Hub (San Diego and DC), Rise Collaborative Workspace (St. Louis), the Hivery (Mill Valley, California), Paper Dolls (Los Angeles), and the Riveter (Seattle) have popped up all over the country. Though these types of spaces are primarily for working on your side hustle (or main hustle), networking, and holding professional meetings, many of them have unflinchingly embraced political engagement and expression as part of their mission. The Wing allowed Women's March organizers to use its space at no cost during the weeks leading up to the march and bused one hundred of its members down to DC on January 21.[9] The Hivery ended up renting six buses to take its members to the San Francisco march.[10]

These spaces, by virtue of being by and for women, end up being political, almost by default. As the Wing co-founder Audrey Gelman put it[11]: "Being a girl is no longer politically neutral. Your identity, whether you like it or not, is now political."

6 STEPS TO FORMING YOUR OWN LADY-CENTERED SPACE

1. THINK ABOUT WHAT YOU NEED. Do you want to create a space for general brainstorming and work? A group that meets monthly to organize around one particular issue? A place where women can share practical strategies for surviving sexism at school or the workplace? Go into this process with at least a loose vision of what you want to get out of it.

2. RECRUIT OTHER LIKE-MINDED LADY FRIENDS. You can't have a lady gang of one. Reach out to your friends at first, then widen the pool. Invite women to invite other women into the fold. When you create a space with a common aim in mind, you may make some really fantastic, talented, and inspiring new friends in the process. At the end of every meeting, make sure to encourage members to bring new people next time!

3. FIND A PHYSICAL SPACE YOU CAN USE. Consistency is a good way to make sure that people keep coming back. Find a classroom, apartment, family room, or public space (a library or park with picnic tables)

where you can meet. If you live in a city that already has a women's co-working space or community center, email the people who run those spaces and see if they'd be willing to help you out.

4. WORK WITH THE OTHERS IN YOUR GROUP TO DEFINE SOME CONCRETE GOALS. Don't meet just for the sake of meeting. After your introductory event, sit down with the people you've invited into this space and really talk about what your goals are. Create a mission statement, write it down, and continue to return to it. Having the occasional informal group therapy session is great—but make sure that you're ultimately making plans to get off your chairs and couches and out into the world.

5. IDENTIFY OTHER GROUPS THAT YOU CAN COLLABORATE WITH AND SUPPORT. Once you've established your group, look beyond yourselves. Research the groups that are already doing the work you want to contribute to in your area, call them up, and ask them what they need. Is it money? Volunteers? Bodies at protests? Whatever they say, use the resources you have to help them out.

6. DON'T FORGET TO HAVE FUN! Celebrate milestones big and small. Dance around. Show affection. Recognize that joy can be radical.

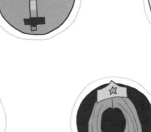

CHAPTER 9

FAKE NEWS, SHMAKE NEWS:
HOW TO SORT THROUGH ALL THE BS

The first time Melissa Zimdars really noticed the proliferation of "fake news" was the day that she got fooled by it.

During the summer of 2016, the assistant professor of communication and media at Merrimack College in Massachusetts was scrolling through her Facebook feed when she came across an article that said Green Bay Packers quarterback Aaron Rodgers had endorsed Democratic presidential candidate Bernie Sanders. Being both a Packers fan and a Bernie fan, she thought, "Hell yeah!" and quickly shared the article.

Shortly afterward she realized that the story wasn't true. She had been duped by a viral hit based on lies—or as Kellyanne Conway would put it, "alternative facts."

After Zimdars fell prey to this "Packer of lies," she started noticing these stories more and more. Some of the "fake news" stories that went viral during 2016 were totally inconsequential—such as a piece that claimed *Star Wars* was being shot in northern Wisconsin[1]—but others were less benign, such as the story that claimed Hillary Clinton was running a child sex ring out of a pizza restaurant,[2] or the one that claimed Florida Democrats wanted to impose "sharia law" on women.[3]

One day, during her Mass Communication class—a lecture course filled with freshmen and sophomores—Zimdars was leading a discussion about media bias. A few of her students commented that liberal news bias wasn't straightforward. They believed that there was a more coordinated conspiracy behind it. To illustrate this point, a student showed her a photo of a *Newsweek* cover that he had found online. The cover featured Hillary Clinton, along with the headline "Madam President."[4] In reality, it was one of *two* covers that *Newsweek* had prepped before November 8, so that they would be prepared to go to press regardless of how the election played out—pretty standard practice for a magazine. But certain fringe right-wing personalities and news outlets had seized upon the image, declaring it evidence that *Newsweek* had colluded with the Clinton campaign to "rig" the election. Once Zimdars explained the context of the image, it made complete sense to her students, but the incident made her realize even more deeply the damage that misleading news can do in the Internet age.

"It just demonstrated to me how quickly and convincingly this kind of information can circulate and have huge effects," Zimdars told me.

So in an effort to help her students more responsibly sort through all the newsy noise they see on social media every day, Zimdars decided to be proactive. She put together a comprehensive Google Doc[5] that included tips for analyzing news sources, as well as a list of "False, Misleading, Clickbait-y, and/or Satirical 'News' Sources," tagged with the type of bias each website might present. The list includes news sources that present totally false news, news sources that present credible news through a political lens, satirical news sources, news sources that promote conspiracy theories, news sources that present junk science, news sources that rely on clickbait headlines (that is, headlines that might exaggerate a point or tease the reader with an answer to get that reader to click into an article), and government-run news sources. Zimdars's list is nuanced and thoughtful, providing real instruction to those who take the time to actually read it thoroughly.

Unsurprisingly, many people didn't. The list went viral, and because of its virality, it became mischaracterized. The nuance was largely lost, as the list was labeled as a "fake news" list, rather than a list of news sources that contains varying types of bias and satire, carefully and specifically labeled. Eventually Zimdars wrote an op-ed in the *Washington Post* about the series of events.[6]

"I've noticed, with some concern, that the same techniques that get people to click on fake or overhyped stories are also being used to get people to read about my own list," she wrote, explaining the original intent of the list: "I wanted to help my students navigate a cluttered, complicated and often overwhelming media environment by alerting them to be skeptical and rigorous at all times."

Skeptical and rigorous: two things that any consumer of media should be. These traits take work—it's easier to just retweet or repost without reading an article than to take the time to read it carefully and to make sure that the conclusions it's drawing aren't spurious or suspect. But being a thoughtful consumer of media is rewarding. Not only does it make you more informed—always a plus—but it also may help restore your faith in the relationship between "the media," so often thought of as a distant, coordinated monolith, in direct conflict with the user, and those who need that media most in times of democratic turmoil.

As Zimdars told me: "What I try to remind my students is that skepticism is healthy. We should all be skeptical of information all the time, right? But it can't become cynicism."

5 TIPS FOR EVERY RESPONSIBLE NEWS READER (THAT MEANS YOU!)

1. **BE YOUR OWN FILTER.** Read your news carefully. If something raises your internal antennas or feels a little fishy, trust that instinct and look into it more.

"We're going to have to really understand instinctively and make our own value judgments of what is right and what smells wrong," media critic and activist Jamia Wilson advises. "We need to see 'alternative facts' for what they are." And if a story *doesn't* seem totally aboveboard? Resist hitting "like."

2. **FACT-CHECK, FACT-CHECK, FACT-CHECK.** Before spreading information on a given topic, make sure you actually have a grasp on that information. And if something feels off, look at reliable sites such as Snopes or PolitiFact to double-check the "truthiness" of the info.

3. **FIND NEWS SOURCES THAT YOU TRUST.** Do your research and decide on a few news outlets that feel steady and reliable to you. Follow them on social media, and read them regularly.

4. **BUT MAKE SURE TO READ WIDELY.** This doesn't just mean oscillating between reading news from outlets that are traditionally categorized as left-wing and those categorized as right-wing—though that could be part of it if that's the variety you're looking for. The most important thing is to simply vary your media diet. No one should get all of her information from one source. After all, the *Boston Globe* may have the best

reporting on one particular topic, while the *Wall Street Journal* or *The Hill* or the *New York Times* delves beautifully into another. No one media organization will teach you everything you need to know about the world.

5. SUPPORT LOCAL NEWS! News organizations should, at their core, be about holding those with the most power responsible for their actions. The best way for media outlets to be able to do this is to (a) have the funding to dedicate enough reporters to a variety of topic areas, and (b) have enough outlets based in a variety of locations across the country or region they cover. There's nothing wrong with having national outlets that are headquartered in New York or DC—it only becomes a problem when you consider that they don't report on local issues, and many local news organizations that *aren't* centered in these places are dying.[7] Find your local paper—if it still exists—and subscribe to it ASAP. Tell your friends and family to do so as well.

CHAPTER 10

○ ○ ○ ○ ○ ○ ○

SELF-CARE,
A.K.A. HOW TO AVOID LOSING YOUR MIND
WHILE YOU'RE CHANGING THE WORLD

C aring for myself is not self-indulgence, it is self-preservation, and that is an act of political warfare," wrote poet, author, and activist Audre Lorde in her 1988 book, *A Burst of Light*.[1]

In the wake of the 2016 presidential election—a moment in which both self-preservation and political warfare felt paramount—the idea of self-care entered the public consciousness more intensely. Google searches for the term spiked during mid-November, as scared and anxious Americans attempted to soothe themselves.[2] And—as is wont to happen with terms coined and used by activists and marginalized groups—once *self-care* became buzzy, it also became somewhat watered down.

A simple Google search turns up lists with headlines such as "19 Items to Buy for Your Mental Health, Because Self-Care Isn't Always Free" and "9 Products That Won't Let You Forget About Self-Care This Year," encouraging readers to purchase a $30 self-care journal or a $65 Jo Malone candle. Don't get me wrong, I love bourgie candles as much as the next girl, and I don't fault anyone for enjoying these products—products can be super fun, and retail therapy feels damn good!—but I'm going to go out on a limb and assume that Audre Lorde was not thinking about going on a high-end bath-product shopping spree when she wrote about self-preservation as political warfare.

☆　☆　☆

In 2012, Lucy McBath's seventeen-year-old son, Jordan Davis, was fatally shot by a man who objected to the loud music he and his friends were playing at a Jacksonville, Florida, gas station. The tragedy rocked Lucy's world and plunged her into an identity crisis. She had been Jordan's mother for nearly twenty years. Who was she now?

Lucy found herself leaning into her Christian faith for solace and talking to God.

"Now that I'm no longer his mother, what do you want me to do with my life?" she asked.

Her answer came in the form of a calling. She sensed that what had happened to Jordan would continue to happen to other young men of color, and that staying silent was no longer an option. She'd never considered herself an activist. Hell, she'd never even been a public speaker. But she had a voice, and she was going to use it.

"I felt like all I needed to do was open my mouth and [see who] would listen to me," she told me. "I felt like God had given me a mandate, and I was going to have to speak out. I felt like even though Jordan is no longer here, physically, I'm still his mother and I still need to parent him and protect him. A part of that was challenging the stand-your-ground laws. I'm going to challenge these laws, and I don't care what it takes. Whoever would be willing to listen to me, whoever would open their doors for me, I was going to [speak to]."

And that is just what she did. And has kept doing.

She began speaking up about gun violence, police brutality, and racism. She told her story and people listened. She launched a national campaign against stand-your-ground laws—which her son's killer used as a defense (he was convicted of first-degree murder in 2014 thanks to Lucy's work). She became the faith and outreach leader for Everytown for Gun Safety and a national spokesperson for Moms Demand Action for Gun Sense in America. She gave a moving address at the 2016 Democratic National Convention, standing shoulder-to-shoulder with other Mothers of the Movement, other mothers who had lost their black children—Trayvon Martin, Eric Garner, Sandra Bland, Mike Brown, Hadiya Pendleton, Dontré Hamilton—at the hands of gun violence and police brutality.[3]

"We're going to keep telling our children's stories and urging you to say their names," she said at the DNC, to those present and the many more watching on television. "We're going to keep building a future where police officers and communities of color work together in mutual respect to keep children, like Jordan, safe. [. . .] And we're also going to keep using our voices and our votes to support leaders, like Hillary Clinton, who will help us protect one another so this club of heartbroken mothers stops growing."

Lucy, if you can't already tell, is an extraordinary woman. She exudes warmth and compassion in a way I have rarely experienced. When we met up for lunch at a restaurant in midtown Manhattan, she greeted me with a full-hearted hug, even though we had only met in person once before. If you sit and talk with Lucy, within ten minutes you feel close to her, and sense that she would fight for your humanity if you were ever in need of her voice.

This unwavering dedication to other human beings also means that sometimes she can forget to take care of herself.

Lucy describes the years immediately after Jordan's death as like being on a train that she couldn't get off. It wasn't until after the 2016 election that she realized she was completely burned out.

"I had planned to take a three-month hiatus, which I did. I was gone after the election and didn't come back, formally, until March," she told me. "It was the best thing I ever did because I really had a chance to figure out and create different ways to do this advocacy. When you're so mired in the work from day to day, I think you have the tendency to lose a lot of the creativity. [Stepping back for a bit] really gave me a chance to sit at home and rest and think about, what does this advocacy look like for me going forward?"

This story of burnout is a common one for activists. After all, the work of creating social change can be emotionally, mentally, and physically grueling. So what's one way to maintain a sense of sanity in the face of daily insanity? Self-care.

For the women I spoke to for this book, who come from various spheres, backgrounds, and geographical locations, self-care is less about relaxation products and more about the intangibles—the space that allows you to take a step back, recharge your soul, and say yes to yourself so that you can continue saying yes to others in effective and creative ways.

I asked extraordinary women how they practiced self-care. Here's what they said.

DEJA FOXX, High School Student and Reproductive Justice Advocate

"To me, self-care means respecting yourself and your efforts. I practice self-care in my busy schedule of activism, academics, and work by doing yoga and spending time with my friends and boyfriend."

LUCY McBATH, Mother of the Movement, Spokesperson for Moms Demand Action for Gun Sense in America, and Faith Outreach Leader for Everytown for Gun Safety

"Weekends, holidays shut down. [At] 6 P.M. phones go off. You have to recognize that you're important. You're important to the movement. It's a matter of preserving your relationships—relationships that you had to people before you became a part of the movement. You've got to nurture them. I did a lot of reading of things outside of gun violence prevention. Just reading stories and reading books and biographies that were not related to the struggle. Going to movies, date night with my husband. It's important to understand and to recognize that you're just a human being, and that this struggle is going to always be here, and it's going to be a long one, and we cannot solve it overnight."

WENDY DAVIS, Former State Senator and Founder of Deeds Not Words

"Family and friends. And I have developed a skill over time that has really served me, which is to compartmentalize, to try to shut down and completely separate myself sometimes from the work, the policies that we care about, and to focus on something right in front of me, whether it's cooking a meal or going on a run or spending time with my baby granddaughter—just really focusing myself in that moment and enjoying and filling myself up by virtue of things that I enjoy. That really leaves your tank a lot fuller for the hard fights to come."

FLAVIA DZODAN, Writer

"If you look at my social media interactions, you will see that there are gaps. There are entire hours, I mean not just when I'm sleeping. Disengaging is the key to self-care for me. I can work on other stuff, but without [the] pressure of having to constantly be available. For me, self-care is not paying attention for a number of hours a day."

HALEY STEVENS, Congressional Candidate

"I have a mantra that's called 'pencils down.' Knowing when to go pencils down, just like when you're at the end of a test. 'This is as much time as I have right now for this. Pencils down.' The best thing is that when I put that pencil down, I can pick it right back up, and I can get back to work. That's not going to go anywhere. I live in a beautiful part of southeastern Michigan where there are some trails, so running and walking; finding that time in the early morning to go for a run or get some exercise in is really helpful. Some of the best advice I got at the beginning of this [campaign] was pencil it in and out. Pencil in. Carve out the time now that you're going to be spending for you."

WINNIE WONG, Founder of People for Bernie

"I think the honest answer is that I don't [practice self-care], but that does not mean I don't think about it. I practice self-care through constantly unpacking my courage. That to me is a form of self-care. It's about understanding and being grateful for my great health, my beautiful apartment, my hot boyfriend, and my pit bull. My hot boyfriend does my laundry for me. This is self-care for me, the fact that he is completely supportive in my work when I'm not available to ever make him macaroni and cheese anymore. This is all self-care to me. Just practicing gratitude for one's privilege is a form of practicing self-care."

CARMEN PEREZ, Women's March National Cochair

"I wake up every morning and I intentionally am grateful for three things. I practice spirituality. I also work out and I try to eat healthy. So I really try to take care of my body, my mind, and my spirit. We're humans, right? So whenever we get death threats or we get people trolling us, of course you're going to have an emotional outburst. But I also know that I have a great, great, great support system. I have a very loving family. I try to model the types of relationships that I ask young people to have. And I also make sure that I keep those people who don't serve me at arm's length."

AMANDA GORMAN, Activist and Youth Poet Laureate of the United States

"I have an interesting self-care regimen, and it often revolves around Pixar movies. I really believe in the power of narratives, and so I hitch onto narratives that speak to me and I'll reread in times of doubt. So whether that's rewatching *Moana* or rereading Harry Potter, I make sure that I take some time to embark on those narratives that help demonstrate what I care about. I meditate, I write, I play with my dog, and then above all I believe in what I call 'Literary Talismans'—they're basically mantras that I repeat to myself in times of anxiety or insecurity, and they remind me of where I've come from, of the people whose shoulders I'm standing on, and what my values are. And so I kind of speak to myself a mantra about being the descendant of slaves, being the descendant of these black freedom fighters, and how I want to further continue this path of deliverance. And I repeat that to myself, and then I feel way more energized about the work that needs to get done. And I always try to get six hugs a day, at least. Hugs are perfect; once you give a hug you cannot stop."

JANAYE INGRAM, National Organizer and Head of Logistics
for Women's March

"For me, self-care is travel. I love to travel. When I feel like life is too much or circumstances, issues, whatever it is, is too much for me, my outlet is through travel. I'm also really closely connected with my family. I see them very often. Those are the two things that for me I really do to practice self-care. It's about allowing myself to really unplug and not necessarily focus on what's happening on the news or what's happening out in the streets."

ELIZABETH WARREN, United States Senator

"Especially in this time of nonstop email, Facebook and Twitter, and round-the-clock news, it can be tough to step back and take a deep breath. But I think it's really important to carve out time for yourself, to recharge and reset. This is going to be a marathon, not a sprint. I'm working on it—and I'm not there yet. I exercise, and I listen to audiobooks. I try not to check email late at night (Trump's 3 A.M. tweets will still be there tomorrow morning). I'm lucky to have a sweetie I'm crazy about, and grandkids and nieces and nephews who remind me why I'm in this fight."

SHANNON WATTS, Founder of Moms Demand Action for Gun Sense in America

"I do a lot of meditation. I do a lot of yoga and working out. I'm married to an amazing, supportive husband. Honestly, my kids are older, that has helped me quite a bit because to have little kids and to be doing this work would be harder. It doesn't mean it's insurmountable. My youngest was twelve when I started Moms [Demand Action] and is almost seventeen now. I think it's really important to recharge and go on vacation. I just climbed Mount Kilimanjaro, and I had zero choice to be completely inaccessible and it was great. The world did not end."

GABRIELLE GORMAN, Filmmaker and YoungArts Winner

"I like to watch a lot of movies from my childhood. I feel like I've been doing that a lot more recently since the election. I'll watch stuff like *The Grants* and *National Treasure* and *Scooby-Doo*. Just sort of simple movies. I think that helps a lot. I try to tell people to find your thing, find something really simple that you can watch. I love this one show, *Psych*, because there's not a lot of drama and it's comedic. I don't know if that's just because I'm a filmmaker that that's the way that I deal with it. I try to have a good balance. If I spend a lot of hours researching one thing that happened and I find myself really going into a hole, then I usually will come up with a battle plan for what I want to do to help that issue, whether it's a meeting, whether it's writing about it or putting it on my list of films to make. Then I will take a break and watch an episode of just some ditsy show."

KAYLA BRIËT, Filmmaker, Composer, and Musician

"I think the hardest thing [about] self-care is [harnessing] the power to say no; to know when it's more important to kind of back down, or pass an opportunity to someone else, or ask for help. Saying no doesn't make you a weak person. It's really important to take that time to gather energy just by being by yourself and to take time to have fun, and to take time to reward yourself for hard work."

SARAH McBRIDE, National Press Secretary for the Human Rights Campaign and LGBTQ Activist

"I think that's something that all of us struggle with. There was a point in my life where I realized, when I was caring for Andy [Sarah's husband who passed away from cancer in 2014], that the only way I could care for him is if I took care of myself, and if I dealt with emotions that I was feeling. I think there was this instinct, particularly as someone who is always so hyperaware of my own privilege, that when Andy was dying of cancer to be like, 'Stop feeling sorry for yourself. You're not dying.' And while that's true and while that's a helpful perspective and while my plight in no way was comparable to Andy's, I still needed to be able to grapple with my own feelings of negativity and fear and sadness. I still had to sleep and have moments of joy and levity. That experience underscored for me the cliché when it comes to self-care—that you can't help other people if you're not helping and taking care of yourself.

For me, honestly, that includes watching a lot of reality television. That is sort of an escape that allows me to—I don't want to say turn my mind off, 'cause there's a lot to unpack in those shows—but allows me to sort of escape in some ways. I have very strong feelings about this, because it's another instance of this punishment of women who engage in levels of self-care through popular culture. Men, when they engage in self-care through consuming popular culture that disproportionately appeals to men, society doesn't blink an eye. But when women engage in, or when any person engages in self-care that deals with popular culture that disproportionately appeals to women, whether it's music or whether it's television, what have you, it's dismissed as superficial, as vapid, as even dangerous to culture. I think people need to set that bullshit aside and allow people to enjoy the shit that they enjoy."

AI-JEN POO, Director of the National Domestic Workers Alliance and Codirector of Caring Across Generations
"I believe in having a practice, something that helps you connect to the essence of who you are and why you do what you do. For me that's yoga and my yoga practice every morning, for some people it's running, some people it's art, other people it's music—whatever it is that helps remind you of who you are and what you stand for. I believe in vacation. Workers fought for weekends and vacation time for a reason, and I believe in taking those and doing it with people that you love because I think that's a big part of how we nourish ourselves for the long haul."

JACKIE CRUZ, Actress and Activist
"I am one of those people who doesn't stop working. But you gotta take care of yourself, or else you can't make a difference. You have to be kind to yourself. I definitely try to eat healthy, [and] I treat my body with respect. And I love to express gratitude. When you don't get an audition or when your world is falling apart, when [Trump] is your new president, I definitely write down everything that I'm grateful for."

MARLO THOMAS, Award-Winning Actress, Author, and Activist
"As an activist, [I find it] important to practice self-care so that you don't burn out. You always want to be rested and ready to step up to the next challenge. And you can't do that without an ample reservoir of energy, passion, good health, goodwill, and good humor. Everyone practices self-care in their own ways. Some meditate, some jog, some get a massage, some take a purposeless walk just to enjoy the smell of the flowers and the company of passersby. I per-

sonally like to exercise, run in the park, lift weights. It gets me out of my 'busy brain' and works off stress as well as pounds. I also love to go to comedy clubs, because laughter always seems to reenergize me. But the bottom line is: it's about taking the kind of care of yourself as you do everyone else in your life. Women are natural caretakers, but the one person we seem not to have time to care for is ourselves. This idea of self-care gives a name to that carelessness. It's important that we feel good, both physically and emotionally—which includes making sure we eat well, get a decent amount of sleep, and don't forget to cuddle up with someone we love. That feels good too."

TINA TCHEN, Former Chief of Staff to First Lady Michelle Obama and Executive Director of the Obama White House Council on Women and Girls
"We live in a time where we are constantly entrenched in messages and media—read this, watch this, share this. Sometimes it's good to turn everything off and to reflect. I think especially in the space of public service, where you're dealing with a multitude of issues and where you're concerned with the well-being of far more than just yourself, it's important to take time to personally react and respond to how certain issues make you feel. In recent months self-care to me has been traveling, catching up with friends and family who I haven't seen as much over the years, and spending time with my children—oh, and binge watching all the shows I haven't had a chance to watch!"

BOB BLAND, Women's March National Cochair
"Honestly, we never really stopped [to take a break] after the march. Because right after was the Muslim ban. And that was just the beginning. The way that I've practiced self-care is that we're very intentional about spending time with our families, and not allowing the most important connections in our lives to suffer. Because what's the point of doing this work if your family comes out of it feeling like they lost you? I try to celebrate even small victories where we

can connect with each other as a community. [The Women's March organizers] may not have known each other when we started, but now we're this very close-knit family of organizers who have been through a once-in-a-lifetime experience together. Organizing the Women's March was like gaining an entire new family."

RAQUEL WILLIS, Organizer and Writer

"For me, self-care isn't something that is so organized or well thought out. I think that when we start to be too structured around self-care, that can actually become work and become less restorative than we would hope, so currently self-care to me is building personal relationships that don't hinge on what's going on in the movement. There's the need for spaces where you can just breathe and people you can just worry about mundane things with, and not have to worry about saving the world, because none of us are superheroes; none of us can run on being invincible. So we need to have those outlets of just normality to branch out into. Also, for me self-care is relaxing. Self-care is watching ridiculous shows on Netflix or Hulu, or it's lighting candles. It's massages, it's lying out in the sun, being out in fresh air. It's reading and writing that doesn't necessarily have anything to do with this capitalist system that we're a part of."

WAZINA ZONDON, Cocreator of *Coming Out Muslim: Radical Acts of Love*

"Some days, [it's] saying no. And actually accepting affirmation and acknowledgment and being proud. Maybe once a year—for me I do it during Ramadan and I do it during birthday times—is looking at the last year and making a list of things I'm so proud of and also thanking the people in my life who help me get there. [. . .] Self-care [is also] watching *The Office* on repeat. I don't watch hard TV. I don't even engage haters anymore. Self-care is no longer reading comments."

JAMIA WILSON, Executive Director and Publisher of the Feminist Press at City University of New York

"For me, it's really about not suffering in silence, connecting with other people in solidarity. Another thing is, as I've gotten older and [been] managing auto-immune illnesses that I have, I feel like my body has created a status for itself that lets me know when I'm working too hard and pushes me to stop. So I really take the time to sleep. I [also] delegate and share opportunities with other people. When I get opportunities to recommend other people to participate in something who might not have that access, to me that is very much a sense of self-care because it makes me feel good to help support other people, but also it helps me feel like I don't have to carry so much. The last thing I would say is I am now near nature—or as near to nature as you can get in New York City—and I take a walk in the park every day. And I just look at ducks and sometimes I just sit by the water, and it's really great. I have this practice that I learned from an indigenous grandmother who I met at a spiritual workshop. And she taught me a ritual of releasing pain into trees by hugging them, and kind of asking the trees permission to unleash what you're carrying into them. So I actually hug trees. It's always funny to tell the conservatives in my life about that. I actually am a tree hugger."

ASHLEY JUDD, Actor, Author, and Activist

"I practice self-care by prioritizing it. I can't transmit that which I do not have. And I love the saying that self-care isn't selfish, it is self-esteem. The patriarchy wants to diminish me in every way, and that includes through sheer exhaustion. Getting enough sleep, which for me is ten and a half hours per night, is really important. Exercise is very important for my brain, as well as for my sense of being physically capable. I am veganish, which is for my health as well as a deeply moral and ethical choice for me. I think reading Audre Lorde about self-care is important to understand why the body is a site of political and social resistance and transformation. I use my voice, write, and find the courage to live my truth in often unfriendly public spaces, which can be made safe by strong female-to-female alliances—which when it comes to self-care are perhaps the coup de grace. Having fun and laughing regularly are a part of self-care . . . . As much as I need community, I also need long stretches of solitude and silence. Being in nature is critical for me—it is both emergency room and church for my spirit. I love to hike and backpack, and especially enjoy solo back-country backpacking in the Appalachian Mountains."

ALICIA GARZA, Cofounder of Black Lives Matter Network and Special Projects Director at the National Domestic Workers Alliance

"For me, self-care is about cultivating my ability to be resilient in the face of oppression and domination. That means I try to be very intentional about cultivating communities that care for me and can hold me accountable to what it takes for me to move toward my vision. Manicures are nice, but that isn't self-care for me. For me, self-care is the spaces that I help to create where I get to access my resilience. That could mean making time for a dance-off with friends, having a support circle, or spending time alone. But I hesitate to only call things that cost money self-care, when so much of what so many of us struggle with is having access to the resources we need to make ends meet."

FEMINIST MIXTAPE

"Run the World (Girls)"
Beyoncé, *4* (2011)

"Salute"
Little Mix, *Salute* (2013)

"Fighter"
Christina Aguilera, *Stripped* (2002)

"The Greatest"
Sia, *This Is Acting* (2016)

WHAT TO LISTEN TO WHEN YOU NEED AN INSPIRATION PICK-ME-UP

"Cold War"
Janelle Monáe, *The ArchAndroid* (2010)

"Formation"
Beyoncé, *Lemonade* (2016)

"Heads Will Roll"
Yeah Yeah Yeahs, *It's Blitz!* (2009)

"Shake It Out"
Florence and the Machine, *Ceremonials* (2011)

"Just a Girl"
No Doubt, *Tragic Kingdom* (1995)

"Nasty"
Janet Jackson, *Control* (1986)

"*Desperado*"
Rihanna, *Anti* (2016)

"*Bulletproof*"
La Roux, *La Roux* (2009)

"*Work It*"
Missy Elliott, *Under Construction* (2002)

"*Dancing on My Own*"
Robyn, *Body Talk Pt. 1* (2010)

"*No Scrubs*"
TLC, *FanMail* (1999)

"*Fuck You*"
Lily Allen, *It's Not Me, It's You* (2009)

"*Cut to the Feeling*"
Carly Rae Jepsen, *Leap! Soundtrack* (2017)

"*L.E.S. Artistes*"
Santigold, *Santogold* (2008)

"*Break Free*"
Ariana Grande, *My Everything* (2014)

"*Feeling Myself*"
Nicki Minaj, *The Pinkprint* (2014)

"*Bad Girls*"
M.I.A., *Matangi* (2013)

"*None of Your Business*"
Salt-N-Pepa, *Very Necessary* (1993)

PS: Beyoncé gets two songs on this list, because she's *Beyoncé*. She could have gotten a hundred.
PPS: Dancing it out to one of these anthems has been known to take the edge off everyday stresses, including (but not limited to) 75 percent of comments Piers Morgan makes; male politicians who tweet their "thoughts and prayers"; the word *bigly*; and the systematic chipping away at your reproductive rights.

WHAT TO WATCH WHEN YOU NEED AN INSPIRATION PICK-ME-UP

Because sometimes you do actually need to sit on your couch—or in your bed, tucked under a mountain of cozy blankets—for a little while.

HIDDEN FIGURES

Learn about the black women who helped make NASA's groundbreaking space program possible. Not only do you get to watch a movie about real-life mathematical superheroes Dorothy Vaughan, Mary Jackson, and Katherine Johnson, but also, every single one of Janelle Monáe's outfits is the stuff vintage sartorial dreams are made of.

THE BLETCHLEY CIRCLE

My favorite genre of TV show is "badass lady detective, preferably with a British accent." This BBC miniseries covers all of those bases. Plus, it's based on the real-life women code breakers who staffed Britain's Bletchley Park during World War II!

THE HANDMAID'S TALE

Okay, so this one isn't exactly uplifting, but Hulu's modern-day adaptation of Margaret Atwood's dystopian tale—a world in which women's rights have been slowly stripped away and fertile women are treated as human hosts for high-status infertile couples—feels just real enough to jolt you into action.

WHAT HAPPENED, MISS SIMONE?

A documentary about the legendary singer and civil rights advocate Nina Simone? That's really all you need to know in order to say hell yes to this one.

PARKS AND RECREATION

Leslie Knope is a dedicated public servant who loves Joe Biden and Galentine's Day. It's hard to get more delightful than that.

ERIN BROCKOVICH

The true story of Erin Brockovich, a single mother who discovers that a gas and electric company has contaminated the water of an entire community in California. Erin, played by Julia Roberts, embarks on a mission to hold them legally accountable. The movie also has great one-liners, like "They're called boobs, Ed." (Which is apparently something the real Erin Brockovich actually said.)

HE NAMED ME MALALA

In 2012, Pakistani teen, writer, and humanitarian Malala Yousafzai was shot and nearly killed by a Taliban gunman in opposition to girls going to school. She survived and went on to become an advocate for girls' educational opportunities and rights around the world. (She also became the youngest Nobel Prize laureate in history.) This 2015 documentary follows her young life and all that she has accomplished.

CONFIRMATION

Anita Hill changed the way we think of workplace sexual harassment in this country. HBO's film adaptation of her story follows Clarence Thomas's 1991 Supreme Court confirmation hearings, during which Hill testified that Thomas had sexually harassed her when she worked for him. She was subsequently dragged through the mud by the press and certain members of Congress.

Thomas was eventually confirmed, but thanks to Hill, we gained a greater national understanding of what sexual harassment looks like in the workplace. In 1991 the Equal Employment Opportunity Commission (EEOC, where Hill had worked under Thomas) saw 3,349 charges filed alleging sexual harassment. One year later, 5,607 were reported. These hearings also ushered in the "Year of the Woman," in which a record-breaking number of women were elected to the Senate and the House.

THELMA AND LOUISE

Geena Davis + Susan Sarandon + Brad Pitt + a disastrous, tragic, and exhilarating road trip that illustrates the deep bonds that form between women = a winner.

MAD MAX: FURY ROAD

Even though this movie is part of the Mad Max franchise, Charlize Theron as the badass, name-taking Imperator Furiosa really steals the show. In a post-apocalyptic world, where women are largely reduced to sexual objects and baby-making vessels, Furiosa rebels against a tyrannical warlord in a quest to save the women said warlord has taken to his harem.

SET IT OFF

Jada Pinkett Smith, Queen Latifah, Vivica A. Fox, and Kimberly Elise walk into a bank . . . and rob it. This "socially conscious heist film" has been compared to *Thelma and Louise* for its incisive look at female solidarity (and structural oppression).

WORKING GIRL

I always have questions while watching *Working Girl*, like "Why does the Big Bad have to be another woman?" and "Why does finding happiness and fulfillment still involve finding a man?" But despite those things, *Working Girl* is pure bliss. Melanie Griffith slays eighties corporate sexism and gets the corner office she deserves. (Plus, the Carly Simon feature song is perfection!)

BUT I'M A CHEERLEADER

Natasha Lyonne plays a cheerleader whose parents suspect she's a lesbian, so they haul her off to a conversion therapy camp called True Directions. Hijinks . . . and love . . . and self-acceptance . . . and empowerment ensue.

JESSICA JONES

This isn't your average superhero show. We first meet Jessica Jones after her (failed and brief) superhero career. She's become a detective with a rather hard edge in New York City. The show deftly deals with issues of sexual assault, domestic abuse, and PTSD, all through the lens of a heightened reality.

SCANDAL

Obviously anything Shonda Rhimes touches is pure gold, but the first few seasons of *Scandal* are particularly inspired. Political fixer Olivia Pope is a hypercompetent "gladiator," even as she guzzles red wine and has an on-and-off affair with the (very dreamy) president of the United States. *Scandal* also exists in a glorious dream world where Republican elites care about Planned Parenthood and immigration reform.

BUFFY THE VAMPIRE SLAYER

Sarah Michelle Gellar's Buffy Summers comes to slay . . . literally. The petite, blond high school student has the weight of the world's evils on her shoulders, and we get to watch her take down vampires, one by one. The show also features a wonderfully subversive ensemble cast while still centering on Buffy. She is not a blond babe who gets killed in the opening scene of a TV show about some heroic dude; *she* is the hero of this story.

MISS FISHER'S MURDER MYSTERIES

1920s Melbourne + a badass lady detective who flouts convention + extended sexual tension = the magic that is Miss Fisher and her murder mysteries. The first episode features Miss Phryne Fisher tracking down the doctor behind an illegal abortion ring—and giving a pretty amazing speech about why abortion being illegal hurts everyone—all while wearing a seriously glamorous outfit. This is Netflix escapism I can really get behind.

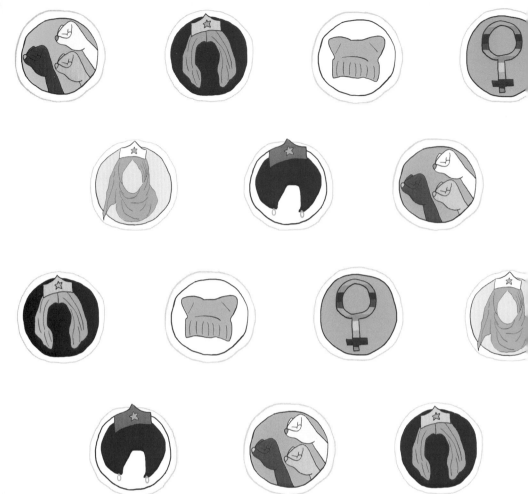

○ ○ ○ ○ ○ ○ ○

CHAPTER 11

ORGANIZATIONS THAT ARE ALREADY DOING THE WORK

The beauty of jumping into the work of creating a more equitable world is that there are many, many, many people who have paved the way. All you have to do is take the time to listen, learn, and follow in their footsteps.

If you've managed to come this far, dear reader, you've got this.

On the following pages you'll find a starter list of organizations that are already doing this hard and important work. Go to their websites and give your time and money whenever you can.

Since the people reading this book live all over the country (and the world), this list primarily focuses on national (U.S.) and international organizations. But it's always good to find the smaller, local groups as well—so I've included a space on pages 119-120 where you can write down the names of any organizations that aren't on this list.

Civil Rights

ASIAN AMERICANS ADVANCING JUSTICE–ASIAN LAW CAUCUS
http://www.advancingjustice-alc.org

AMERICAN CIVIL LIBERTIES UNION (ACLU)
https://www.aclu.org

COUNCIL ON AMERICAN-ISLAMIC RELATIONS (CAIR)
https://www.cair.com

LAWYERS' COMMITTEE FOR CIVIL RIGHTS UNDER LAW
https://lawyerscommittee.org

MEXICAN AMERICAN LEGAL DEFENSE AND EDUCATIONAL FUND (MALDEF)
http://www.maldef.org

NAACP LEGAL DEFENSE FUND
http://www.naacpldf.org

Criminal Justice Reform

#CUT50
https://www.cut50.org

ELLA BAKER CENTER FOR HUMAN RIGHTS
http://www.ellabakercenter.org

EQUAL JUSTICE INITIATIVE
https://eji.org

INNOCENCE PROJECT
https://www.innocenceproject.org

RESTORATIVE JUSTICE FOR OAKLAND YOUTH
http://rjoyoakland.org

THE SENTENCING PROJECT
http://www.sentencingproject.org

ZEHR INSTITUTE FOR RESTORATIVE JUSTICE
http://zehr-institute.org/about

Disability Rights

ADAPT
http://adapt.org

DISABILITY RIGHTS ADVOCATES
http://dralegal.org/about

DISABILITY RIGHTS EDUCATION & DEFENSE FUND
https://dredf.org

Electoral Politics

HIGHER HEIGHTS
http://www.higherheightsforamerica.org

IGNITE
http://www.ignitenational.org

RUN FOR SOMETHING
https://www.runforsomething.net

SHE SHOULD RUN
http://www.sheshouldrun.org

SWING LEFT
https://swingleft.org

Environmental Protection

AMERICAN RIVERS
https://www.americanrivers.org

EARTHJUSTICE
http://earthjustice.org

ENVIRONMENTAL DEFENSE FUND
https://www.edf.org

THE NATURE CONSERVANCY
https://www.nature.org

NATURAL RESOURCES DEFENSE COUNCIL (NRDC)
https://www.nrdc.org

SIERRA CLUB
http://www.sierraclub.org

TRUST FOR PUBLIC LAND
https://www.tpl.org

Fighting Hate

ANTI-DEFAMATION LEAGUE (ADL)
https://www.adl.org

PLANTING PEACE
https://www.plantingpeace.org

SOUTHERN POVERTY LAW CENTER
https://www.splcenter.org

Gun Violence

AMERICANS FOR RESPONSIBLE SOLUTIONS
http://americansforresponsiblesolutions.org/stand-with-gabby

EVERYTOWN FOR GUN SAFETY
https://everytown.org

MOMS DEMAND ACTION FOR GUN SENSE IN AMERICA
https://momsdemandaction.org

VIOLENCE POLICY CENTER
http://www.vpc.org

Immigration and Refugee Rights

ALIANZA AMERICAS
http://www.alianzaamericas.org

BLACK ALLIANCE FOR JUST IMMIGRATION (BAJI)
http://blackalliance.org

FAMILIES FOR FREEDOM
http://familiesforfreedom.org

INTERNATIONAL RESCUE COMMITTEE (IRC)
https://www.rescue.org

KIDS IN NEED OF DEFENSE (KIND)
https://supportkind.org

MARIPOSAS SIN FRONTERAS
https://mariposassinfronteras.org

NATIONAL IMMIGRATION LAW CENTER
https://www.nilc.org

NORTHWEST IMMIGRANT RIGHTS PROJECT
https://www.nwirp.org

TAHIRIH JUSTICE CENTER
http://www.tahirih.org

UNDOCUBLACK NETWORK
http://undocublack.org

UNITED WE DREAM
https://unitedwedream.org

THE YOUNG CENTER FOR IMMIGRANT CHILDREN'S RIGHTS
http://theyoungcenter.org

LGBTQ Rights

THE AUDRE LORDE PROJECT
https://alp.org

GLAAD
https://www.glaad.org

HUMAN RIGHTS CAMPAIGN (HRC)
http://www.hrc.org

LAMBDA LEGAL
https://www.lambdalegal.org

NATIONAL CENTER FOR TRANSGENDER EQUALITY
http://www.transequality.org

PFLAG
https://www.pflag.org

SYLVIA RIVERA LAW PROJECT
https://srlp.org

TRANS LIFELINE
https://www.translifeline.org

THE TREVOR PROJECT
http://www.thetrevorproject.org

Press Freedom

COMMITTEE TO PROTECT JOURNALISTS
https://cpj.org

THE MARSHALL PROJECT
https://www.themarshallproject.org

REPORTERS COMMITTEE FOR FREEDOM OF THE PRESS
https://www.rcfp.org

Racial Justice

ADVANCEMENT PROJECT
http://www.advancementproject.org

BLACK LIVES MATTER
http://blacklivesmatter.com

BLACK YOUTH PROJECT 100 (BYP100)
http://byp100.org

COLOR OF CHANGE
https://www.colorofchange.org

MILLION HOODIES MOVEMENT FOR JUSTICE
http://millionhoodies.net

NATIONAL ASSOCIATION FOR THE ADVANCEMENT OF COLORED PEOPLE (NAACP)
http://www.naacp.org

RACE FORWARD: THE CENTER FOR RACIAL JUSTICE INNOVATION
https://www.raceforward.org

SHOWING UP FOR RACIAL JUSTICE (SURJ)
http://www.showingupforracialjustice.org

Reproductive Rights

CENTER FOR REPRODUCTIVE RIGHTS
https://www.reproductiverights.org

NARAL PRO-CHOICE AMERICA
https://www.prochoiceamerica.org

NATIONAL ABORTION FEDERATION
https://prochoice.org

NATIONAL LATINA INSTITUTE FOR REPRODUCTIVE HEALTH
http://www.latinainstitute.org/en

NATIONAL NETWORK OF ABORTION FUNDS
https://abortionfunds.org

NATIONAL WOMEN'S HEALTH NETWORK
https://www.nwhn.org

PLANNED PARENTHOOD
https://www.plannedparenthood.org

REPRODUCTIVE HEALTH ACCESS NETWORK
http://www.reproductiveaccess.org

Sexual and Domestic Violence

END RAPE ON CAMPUS
http://endrapeoncampus.org

FUTURES WITHOUT VIOLENCE
https://www.futureswithoutviolence.org

KNOW YOUR IX
https://www.knowyourix.org

NATIONAL COALITION AGAINST DOMESTIC VIOLENCE
http://www.ncadv.org

NATIONAL SEXUAL VIOLENCE RESOURCE CENTER (NSVRC)
http://www.nsvrc.org

RAPE, ABUSE & INCEST NATIONAL NETWORK (RAINN)
https://www.rainn.org

Women's and Girls' Rights

AMERICAN ASSOCIATION OF UNIVERSITY WOMEN (AAUW)
http://www.aauw.org

ASSOCIATION FOR WOMEN'S RIGHTS IN DEVELOPMENT (AWID)
https://www.awid.org

BLACK GIRLS ROCK!
http://www.blackgirlsrockinc.com

GIRLS INC.
http://www.girlsinc.org

MALALA FUND
https://www.malala.org

MS. FOUNDATION FOR WOMEN
https://forwomen.org

NATIONAL ORGANIZATION FOR WOMEN (NOW)
http://now.org

NATIONAL WOMEN'S LAW CENTER
https://nwlc.org

ULTRAVIOLET
https://weareultraviolet.org

WOMEN'S MARCH
https://www.womensmarch.com

Workers' Rights

JOBS WITH JUSTICE
http://www.jwj.org

NATIONAL DOMESTIC WORKERS ALLIANCE
https://www.domesticworkers.org

IMPORTANT ⦂AF⦂ ORGANIZATIONS
IN YOUR AREA

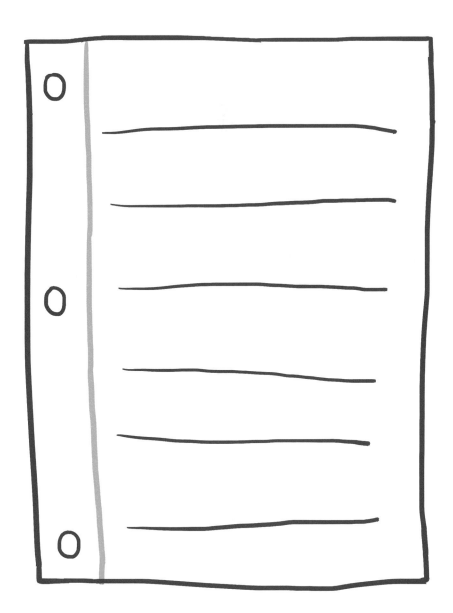

ACKNOWLEDGMENTS

Whenever I'd thought about the Nora Ephron-ism "Everything is copy," I'd thought about turning my personal lemons into lemonade: a bad breakup, a crappy concert, the time a mouse got trapped in my apartment and I hid in my kitchen until a friend came to rescue me, and so on.

I never imagined that "the copy" of my first book would be inspired by the unfulfilled promise of our first woman president—and the subsequent rise of a women-led resistance. I would so much rather live in a world where Hillary Clinton was president and I hadn't written a book. And yet… here we are. Since I can't create an alternate reality, and I did, somehow, manage to write a book, I must thank all of the very brilliant people who helped make it happen.

Eva Hill, there is no better collaborator than you. Your talent is unparalleled, and you brought joy, light, and life to my words. You are also one of the most positive, kind people I've ever encountered. Thank goodness for your warmth and patience. Somehow you never got annoyed at me and Emma when we sent you yet another email. Basically, you're an angel.

ACKNOWLEDGMENTS

Emma Brodie, this project would quite literally not have happened without you. You told me to write a book for years—and for years I laughed in your face and made excuses. I am so damn happy that when I finally did work up the courage to commit to a project like this, it was with you as my copilot. You shaped *Girl's Guide* from a collection of thoughts into an actual (and hopefully fairly coherent!) book. You are a beautiful editor and an equally beautiful friend.

Of course, I need to thank my incredible team at HarperCollins. Leah Carlson-Stanisic and Mumtaz Mustafa, you made *Girl's Guide* beautiful, on the literal inside and out. Libby Collins and Molly Waxman, thank you so much for fielding all of my phone calls and emails, and for helping me make sure this book reaches the audience it is intended for. Special thanks to Susan Kosko, Jeanie Lee, Cassie Jones, Jennifer Hart, and Liate Stehlik. Words cannot express what your hustle and enthusiasm on behalf of this book has meant to me.

Thank you to my family—especially my mom, dad, brother, and grandparents—for raising me to trust my own voice, listen to others, and give a fuck when I see injustice in the world. And thank you for sending me to Habonim Dror Camp Moshava, where I got to spend my formative years reading Eve Ensler and talking about social justice and meeting other kids who also grew up giving a fuck.

I have to recognize my friends and colleagues (hey there, Lady Corner!) who read early drafts, gave me invaluable feedback, made spreadsheets and playlists, fielded my anxious phone calls, took me to get a drink when I desperately needed one, shared their contacts, brainstormed ways to get the book out into the world, and filled in the gaps at work so I could actually take book leave and write this damn thing: Julie Alvin, Lena Auerbuch Anderson, Kristina Apgar, Jessie Assimon, Kate Auletta, Zeba Blay, Erin Darke, Kate Dearing, Claire Fallon, Lindsey Green, Jessica Goodman, Jenavieve Hatch, Kate Hutchison, Sami Kriegstein, Caroline

Modarressy-Tehrani, Emma Mustich, Sarah Novatt, Nick Offenberg, Catherine Pearson, Liz Plank, Jess Samakow, Dana Sherne, Laura Stampler, Lauren Stephenson, Adina Tabor, Taylor Trudon, Alanna Vagianos, and Brittany Wallace. Thank you, thank you, thank you.

To the lady bosses who helped launch my career—Margaret Wheeler Johnson, Laura Schocker, Lori Leibovich, Farah Miller, Lori Fradkin, Lisa Belkin, Arianna Huffington—you made me believe that I could actually make this whole professional-writer thing work.

A special shout-out to The Wing and its cofounder Audrey Gelman (and all of the Wing women who chatted with me during my long writing days) for giving me a magical space to do my writing in. I think I might have curled into a ball and given up halfway through if I hadn't been working from the most delightful place in all of New York City, surrounded by a coven of inspiring women.

Finally, a massive thank-you to all of the incredible women who spoke to me for this book. You are my greatest inspiration, and your trailblazing work is the reason we can all still get up in the morning and soldier on in the face of unthinkable darkness. And to all of the women of yesterday who dedicated their lives to creating opportunities for the girls and women of today, I am forever in your debt and will spend *my* life trying to make you proud.

NOTES

INTRODUCTION

1   Clara Lemlich Shavelson, "Remembering the Waistmakers General Strike, 1909," *Jewish Currents*, 1982, http://jewishcurrents.org/wp-content/uploads/2010/02/Lemlich1.pdf.

2   Tony Michels, "Uprising of 20,000," Jewish Women's Archive, https://jwa.org/encyclopedia/article/uprising-of-20000-1909.

3   Melanie Crowder, *Audacity* (New York: Philomel Books, 2015).

4   Michels, "Uprising."

5   Annelise Orleck, *Common Sense and a Little Fire: Women and Working-Class Politics in the United States, 1900–1965* (Chapel Hill: University of North Carolina Press, 1995), 53.

6   Carol Berkin, "Angelina and Sarah Grimke: Abolitionist Sisters," Gilder Lehrman Institute of American History, https://www.gilderlehrman.org/history-by-era/slavery-and-anti-slavery/essays/angelina-and-sarah-grimke-abolitionist-sisters.

7   Raul A. Reyes, "A Forgotten Latina Trailblazer: LGBT Activist Sylvia Rivera," NBC News, October 6, 2015, http://www.nbcnews.com/news/latino/forgotten-latina-trailblazer-lgbt-activist-sylvia-rivera-n438586.

8   Gloria Steinem, adapted from articles published in *Ms.*, July 1978 and July/August 1982, reprinted in *Outrageous Acts and Everyday Rebellions* (New York: New American Library, 1983).

9   Ariel Edwards-Levy, "Progressive Activism Has Surged Since Donald Trump Took Office," HuffPost, March 30, 2017, http://www.huffingtonpost.com/entry/progressive-activism-surge-donald-trump-took-office_us_58dd8950e4b0e6ac7093b3c1.

10 Tim Marcin, "Black Lives Matter Four Years Later: Under Trump, Movement Is Under Attack," *Newsweek*, July 13, 2017, http://www.newsweek.com/black-lives-matter-4-year-anniversary-under-donald-trump-movement-faces-new-636000.

CHAPTER 1: THERE'S NO TIME LIKE THE PRESENT TO GIVE ALL THE F**KS

1   Christine Wang and Dan Mangan, "CBO: Obamacare Repeal Bill Would Raise Number of Uninsured by 32 million by 2026," CNBC, July 19, 2017, http://www.cnbc.com/2017/07/19/cbo-obamacare-repeal-bill-would-raise-number-of-uninsured-by-27-million-by-2020.html.

2   Mary Emily O'Hara, "Trump Pulls Back Obama-Era Protections for Women Workers," NBC News, April 3, 2017, http://www.nbcnews.com/news/us-news/trump-pulls-back-obama-era-protections-women-workers-n741041.

3   Philip Rucker, "Trump Touts Recent Immigration Raids, Calls Them a 'Military Operation,'" *Washington Post*, February 23, 2017, https://www.washingtonpost.com/news/post-politics/wp/2017/02/23/trump-touts-recent-immigration-raids-calls-them-a-military-operation/?utm_term=.629316114935.

4   Laura Bassett, "Donald Trump Drastically Expands 'Global Gag Rule' on Abortion," HuffPost, May 15, 2017, http://www.huffingtonpost.com/entry/donald-trump-global-abortion-policy_us_5919bacae4b0031e737f382e.

5   Sonam Sheth, "Here's Every Law Trump Has Signed in His First 100 Days," *Business Insider*, April 28, 2017, http://www.businessinsider.com/trump-100-days-congress-regulations-laws-signed-repeal-obama-2017-4.

6   Erica Chenoweth and Jeremy Pressman, "This Is What We Learned by Counting the Women's Marches," *Washington Post*, February 7, 2017, https://www.washingtonpost.com/news/monkey-cage/wp/2017/02/07/this-is-what-we-learned-by-counting-the-womens-marches/?utm_term=.5d34f3a1a7e8.

7   Erin Loos Cutraro, "Thousands of Women Are Geared to Run for Elected Office—Now What?," The Hill, July 19, 2017, http://thehill.com/blogs/pundits-blog/campaign/342604-thousands-of-women-want-to-run-for-office-now-what.

CHAPTER 3: ON GETTING ANGRY: THE POWER OF PROTEST

1   Jeffrey Schmalz, "Gay Marchers Throng Mall in Appeal for Rights," *New York Times*, April 26, 1993, http://www.nytimes.com/1993/04/26/us/march-for-gay-rights-gay-marchers-throng-mall-in-appeal-for-rights.html.

2   Emma Gray, "Politically Engaged Young Women Will Be the Legacy of the Women's March," HuffPost, January 23, 2017, http://www.huffingtonpost.com/entry/womens-march-legacy_us_587a3dc1e4b0e58057ff1ebd.

3   Emma Gray and Jessica Samakow, "Parents for Occupy Wall Street Family Sleepover: 500 Parents and Children Gather in Zuccotti Park," HuffPost, Octo-

ber 22, 2011, http://www.huffingtonpost.com/2011/10/22/occupy-wall-street-family
-sleepover_n_1026461.html.

4   Emma Gray, Catherine Pearson, and Damon Dahlen, "Listen to 13 Women Share the
Powerful Reasons They Marched," HuffPost, January 21, 2017, updated March 22,
2017, http://www.huffingtonpost.com/entry/photos-of-women-and-the-powerful
-reasons-they-march_us_5883d396e4b0e3a735698a12.

5   Christopher Klein, "Remembering 'Bloody Sunday,'" History, March 6, 2015,
http://www.history.com/news/selmas-bloody-sunday-50-years-ago.

6   Klein, "Remembering."

7   "Diane Nash, Civil Rights Movement Leader, Reflects on Selma," ABC7, March 5,
2015, http://abc7chicago.com/society/diane-nash-civil-rights-movement-leader
-reflects-on-selma/546052/.

8   Roy Reed, "Incident at Selma," *New York Times*, March 9, 1965, http://query
.nytimes.com/mem/archive-free/pdf?res=9806E6DA133DEE3ABC4153DF
B566838E679EDE.

9   Don Lemon, "Teen Faces Off with Senator at Town Hall," CNN Tonight, April 15,
2016, http://www.cnn.com/videos/politics/2017/04/15/16-year-old-flake-town
-hall-planned-parenthood-sot-ctn.cnn

CHAPTER 4: DEAR WHITE LADIES: A NOTE ON INTERSECTIONALITY

1   "For Stanton, All Women Were Not Created Equal," NPR, *Morning Edition*, July
31, 2011, http://www.npr.org/2011/07/13/137681070/for-stanton-all-women-were
-not-created-equal.

2   Bim Adewunmi, "Kimberlé Crenshaw on Intersectionality: 'I Wanted to Come
Up with an Everyday Metaphor That Anyone Could Use,'" *New Statesman*, April
2, 2014, http://www.newstatesman.com/lifestyle/2014/04/kimberl-crenshaw
-intersectionality-i-wanted-come-everyday-metaphor-anyone-could.

3   Adewunmi, "Kimberlé Crenshaw."

4   Alanna Vagianos, "Read the Women's March on Washington's Beautifully
Intersectional Platform," HuffPost, January 13, 2017, http://www.huffingtonpost
.com/entry/read-the-womens-march-on-washingtons-beautifully-intersectional
-policy-platform_us_5878e0e8e4b0e58057fe4c4b.

CHAPTER 5: YOUR STORY MATTERS (AND OTHER THINGS THAT SOUND TRITE BUT ARE TRUE)

1   Coming Out Muslim, http://comingoutmuslim.com.

2   Maya Dusenberry, "Can Storytelling Help Destroy Abortion Stigma?," *Pacific Standard*, February 5, 2015, https://psmag.com/social-justice/abortion-storytelling-may-reduce-stigma.

3   T. F. Pettigrew and L. R. Tropp, "A Meta-analytic Test of Intergroup Contact Theory," *Journal of Personal and Social Psychology* 90, no. 5 (May 2006): 761–83, https://www.ncbi.nlm.nih.gov/pubmed/16737372.

4   Advocates for Youth, 1 in 3 Campaign, http://www.1in3campaign.org/about.

5   Shout Your Abortion, https://shoutyourabortion.com.

6   Sarah McBride, "Forever and Ever: Losing My Husband at 24," Medium, August 24, 2015, https://medium.com/@SarahEMcBride/forever-and-ever-losing-my-husband-at-24-800af5a6c53d.

7   McBride, "Forever."

CHAPTER 8: HOW TO STOP WATCHING NETFLIX, GET OFF YOUR COUCH, AND GET SH*T DONE NOW

1   Emma Gray, "Clinton's Loss Has Motivated Thousands to Consider Running for Office," HuffPost, December 12, 2016, http://www.huffingtonpost.com/entry/hillary-clintons-loss-has-motivated-thousands-of-women-to-consider-running-for-office_us_584eeb33e4b04c8e2bb0d0e7.

2   Rebecca Shapiro, "Donald Trump's Presidency Has Inspired 11,000 Women to Run for Office," HuffPost, April 24, 2017, http://www.huffingtonpost.com/entry/donald-trumps-presidency-has-inspired-11000-women-to-run-for-office_us_58fd863ae4b06b9cb917d111.

3   Daring Discussions, Daring Discussions Tool Kit, http://daringdiscussions.com/wp-content/uploads/2017/05/Daring-Discussions_Tool-Kit.pdf.

CHAPTER 8: LADY CLUBS AND COVENS: WHERE THE REAL WORK (AND MAGIC) HAPPENS

1   Carol Hanisch, "Women's Liberation Consciousness-Raising: Then and Now," On the Issues, Spring 2010, http://www.ontheissuesmagazine.com/2010spring/2010spring_Hanisch.php.

2   The Chicago Women's Liberation Union, "How to Start Your Own Consciousness-Raising Group," CWLU Herstory Website Archive, 1971, https://web.archive.org/web/20040212200503/http://www.cwluherstory.com/CWLUArchive/crcwlu.html.

3   Star Ziv, "'Good Girls Revolt': The Feminist Legacy of a *Newsweek* Lawsuit," *Newsweek*, October 23, 2016, http://www.newsweek.com/good-girls-revolt-legacy-newsweek-lawsuit-512224.

4   EMW Women's Surgical Center, http://www.emwwomens.com.

5   "Sunday Brunch with Higher Heights," Higher Heights, http://www.higher heightsforamerica.org/sunday_brunch.

6   The Broad Room, https://www.thebroadroomnyc.com/about.

7   Elaine Pofeldt, "Freelancers Now Make Up 35% of U.S. Workforce," *Forbes*, October 6, 2016, https://www.forbes.com/sites/elainepofeldt/2016/10/06/new-survey -freelance-economy-shows-rapid-growth/#3498914e7c3f.

8   Nicole Dow, "Who Run the World?: Girls Do at These 8 Co-Working Spaces for Women," The Penny Hoarder, March 23, 2017, https://www.thepennyhoarder .com/jobs-making-money/women-focused-co-working-spaces.

9   Lizzy Goodman, "Audrey Gelman's The Wing Is the Feminist Answer to Co-Working Spaces," *Elle*, March 24, 2017, http://www.elle.com/culture/a43609/the -wing-audrey-gelman.

10   Goodman, "The Wing."

11   Goodman, "The Wing."

CHAPTER 9: FAKE NEWS, SHMAKE NEWS: HOW TO SORT THROUGH ALL THE BS

1   Matt Wild, "No, the Next 'Star Wars' Movie Will NOT Be Filmed Near Green Bay," *Milwaukee Record*, April 25, 2016, http://milwaukeerecord.com/film/no-next-star -wars-movie-will-not-filmed-near-green-bay.

2   Aric Jenkins, "'Pizzagate' Gunman Pleads Guilty to Comet Ping Pong Shooting," *Time*, March 24, 2017, http://time.com/4712875/pizzagate-edgar-maddison-welch -guilty-comet-ping-pong.

3   Amy Sherman, "Trump Security Adviser Pick Michael Flynn Repeated Wildly Wrong Claim about FL Democrats, Sharia Law," PolitiFact, November 22, 2016, http://www.politifact.com/florida/article/2016/nov/22/donald-trumps-security -adviser-pick-michael-flynn-.

4   "'Madam President' Hillary Clinton *Newsweek* Cover," Snopes, November 7, 2016, http://www.snopes.com/clinton-newsweek-cover.

5   Ananya Bhattacharya, "Here's a Handy Cheat Sheet of False and Misleading 'News' Sites," Quartz, November 17, 2016, https://qz.com/839160/heres-a-handy-cheat -sheet-of-false-and-misleading-news-sites.

6   Melissa Zimdars, "My Fake News List Went Viral: But Made-Up Stories Are Only Part of the Problem," *Washington Post*, November 18, 2016, https://www .washingtonpost.com/posteverything/wp/2016/11/18/my-fake-news-list

-went-viral-but-made-up-stories-are-only-part-of-the-problem/?utm_term=
.ab323de23466.

7   David Silverberg, "This Map Shows Where and Why Local Newspapers Are Shutting Down," Motherboard, June 29, 2016, https://motherboard.vice.com/en_us/article /bmv733/ryerson-journalism-local-news-map-media-canada.

CHAPTER 10: SELF-CARE, A.K.A. HOW TO AVOID LOSING YOUR MIND WHILE YOU'RE CHANGING THE WORLD

1   Sarah Mirk, "Audre Lorde Thought of Self-Care as an 'Act of Political Warfare,'" Bitch Media, February 18, 2016, https://www.bitchmedia.org/article/audre-lorde -thought-self-care-act-political-warfare.

2   Marisa Meltzer, "Soak, Steam, Spritz: It's All Self-Care," *New York Times*, December 10, 2016, https://www.nytimes.com/2016/12/10/fashion/post-election-anxiety -self-care.html.

3   "Full Speech: 'Mothers of the Movement' Address 2016 DNC," Fox News, July 27, 2016, http://video.foxnews.com/v/5052324825001/?#sp=show-clips.